P9-BZS-512

How to Get a Job on
WALL
STREET

How to Get a Job on WALL STREET

Proven Ways to Land a
High-Paying, High-Powered Job

Scott Hoover

 New York   Chicago   San Francisco   Lisbon   London   Madrid   Mexico City
Milan   New Delhi   San Juan   Seoul   Singapore   Sydney   Toronto

The **McGraw·Hill** Companies

Copyright © 2012 by The McGraw-Hill Companies, Inc. All rights reserved. Printed in the United States of America. Except as permitted under the United States Copyright Act of 1976, no part of this publication may be reproduced or distributed in any form or by any means, or stored in a data base or retrieval system, without the prior written permission of the publisher.

1 2 3 4 5 6 7 8 9 0   DOC/DOC   1 6 5 4 3 2 1

ISBN: 978-0-07-177853-4
MHID: 0-07-177853-5

e-ISBN 978-0-07-177855-8
e-MHID 0-07-177855-1

This publication is designed to provide accurate and authoritative information in regard to the subject matter covered. It is sold with the understanding that neither the author nor the publisher is engaged in rendering legal, accounting, securities trading, or other professional service. If legal advice or other expert assistance is required, the services of a competent professional person should be sought.

  –From a Declaration of Principles Jointly Adopted by a Committee of the American Bar Association and a Committee of Publishers and Associations

McGraw-Hill books are available at special quantity discounts to use as premiums and sales promotions or for use in corporate training programs. To contact a representative, please e-mail us at bulksales@mcgraw-hill.com.

This book is printed on acid-free paper.

CONTENTS

....▶

PREFACE

....▶

As a professor at Washington and Lee University (W&L) for the last 11 years, I have worked with numerous students who are interested in a long-term career in finance and with alumni who are looking to take the next step in their careers in finance. I also have worked with finance professionals and recruiters at every major investment bank and many other financial services firms in an effort to understand better how to place W&L students in the best finance jobs. Many of my students have sought to begin their careers on Wall Street, where they can work with the very brightest peers and develop skills and contacts that will benefit them for the rest of their lives. W&L has the distinction of being the only top 25 liberal arts school with a business program, and so it produces a unique brand of student. That uniqueness, coupled with the small size of the school, historically meant that W&L students faced a bit of an uphill battle in trying to land jobs on Wall Street. Those students had to network actively with friends and alumni on Wall Street to have their résumés reviewed and had to know finance inside and out to get through the interview process. For W&L students, this task has become a bit easier over time because the number of alumni on Wall Street has grown dramatically. W&L is now a core school at several major investment banks, and this gives its students easy access to the interviewing process. At other major investment banks, however, W&L students still face an uphill battle to be recognized.

Over the last 11 years, literally hundreds of students have spent time in my office seeking advice on how to land a job in financial services. Although those students have asked an incredibly broad array of questions, their questions typically fall into three categories: (1) questions related to how get an interview, (2) questions related to how to succeed in interviews, and (3) questions related to how to manage the offer process. After answering the same questions over and over each year, it became clear to me that there was a need for a book focused specifically on how to land a job on Wall Street. Although there are other resources available to students (I will mention a few of them later in the book), I found no single resource that was both complete and practical in laying out what it takes to get a job on Wall Street. That is where this book comes in.

ACKNOWLEDGMENTS

....▶

There are numerous people I should probably thank, but in the interests of time and space I will name just a few. The origins of this book lie with Nick Sayers, a former student who went into investment banking and now works in Chicago in the private equity sector. After struggling through the job market process with little guidance, Nick took the time to write a brief manuscript detailing his experiences. His hope was to make the process easier and more understandable for the students who came after him. That manuscript helped countless students over the subsequent years and provided me with a conviction that a broader manuscript on the subject would be worthwhile. Both John Church at Wells Fargo and Ken Lang at JPMorgan have provided me with a lot more insight over the years than they probably realize. Hiter Harris and Stevie Toepke at Harris Williams graciously shared their corporate hiring strategies with me and in doing so gave me a great deal of insight into how they compete (quite successfully) against the bulge bracket firms. Over the years, Matt Bevin (who has been a strong and articulate advocate of integrity in the financial services industry—hence the name of his firm: Integrity Asset Management) also provided meaningful insight into the hiring process. Others have been more than a bit helpful, including Alex Appel, Brian Castleberry, Don Childress, Natalie Day, Will Flynn, John Gammage, Steve Hostetler, Ross Jagar, John Jensen, Sarah Ann Knier, Jess Lipsey, Samantha McLemore, Bill Miller, Keith Pelt, Bob Sadler, Akshat Shah, Mike Stefan, and Erik Welle. Perhaps as much as any others, I need to thank the numerous former students who have gone through the interview process over the years and then shared their experiences with me. Finally, I would be remiss not to thank my wife, Annalie, who over the years has put up with a lot of late nights working and the stress that comes with that.

INTRODUCTION

....▶

Investment banking jobs are notorious for requiring long work hours at odd times, with employers expecting that young analysts will work at a moment's notice whenever needed. Still, those jobs can be quite rewarding financially because they often lead to more senior jobs that require fewer hours and pay far more. Thus, getting that first finance job is an important step for those interested in a long-term career in finance.

This book is an attempt to distill the vast amount of information on careers in finance down to a few simple ideas that will help even candidates with little financial knowledge successfully compete for top-tier jobs at major financial services companies. It is written with investment banking candidates in mind, but the advice it presents applies broadly to virtually all careers in financial services. Simply put, candidates who are capable of getting jobs in investment banking are typically well qualified to get jobs elsewhere in financial services.

We will go into more detail later, but in simple terms a job candidate should spend time learning about (1) the role of finance in society and how he or she might fit into that world, (2) the basic concepts at the core of finance, (3) the basic economic concepts that influence financial events, and (4) the firm at which the candidate is seeking a job. We also will discuss résumés and basic interviewing skills that apply to all job seekers, not just those looking for jobs in finance.

Before we begin, it is worth spending a few moments to dispel two common misconceptions about investment banks. First, the perception among many people interested in a financial services career is that all finance jobs in an investment bank require the same long hours and have the same accompanying stress. That is decidedly not the case. Investment banks offer finance-related jobs in a variety of areas, with some of those jobs requiring fewer, more predictable hours while making it possible for successful job candidates to advance quickly to high-paying positions. Therefore, students who do not believe they are well suited to the stereotypical investment banking job should keep an open mind about other jobs in financial services. Second, the perception among many students is that it is very difficult for majors in fields other than business, accounting, and economics to compete for banking jobs. Quite the opposite is true. Banks actively seek out candidates with other majors because it allows them to diversify their employee bases intellectually. Banks routinely ask about students not just from technical fields such as engineering, computer science, and math but also from fields such as psychology in which students seek to understand human behavior and fields such as English in which students learn to be exceptional writers.

This book is written under the assumption that readers have at least a basic knowledge of finance and accounting. For those without that knowledge, a glossary at the end of the book defines many of the relevant terms commonly used in the finance world. Words or phrases that appear in boldface in the text also appear in the glossary. In the text, sample interview questions that are taken from actual interviews of candidates seeking jobs in the financial services industry are denoted SIQ. Those interested in pursuing a career in finance should pay careful attention to these questions as they provide insight into what interviewers are trying to achieve and how they will phrase questions to meet their objectives. Having said that, perhaps the single worst way to prepare for an interview is to memorize "good" answers to questions. The financial world is full of very bright and perceptive people. When conducting interviews, these people tend to go well beyond the candidate's initial response, particularly if they suspect that the answer was a canned one. The best way to succeed in an interview is not to memorize good answers to expected questions but to understand the relevant material. The simplest way to get this sort of understanding is to ask yourself continually "Why?" as you prepare for interviews. For example, you might ask, "Why do we add back depreciation in the free cash flow equation?" "Why is it important to understand mathematical expectations if you are interviewing for a sales and trading position?" and "Why is debt generally cheaper than equity?" Candidates who understand *why* basic ideas are important tend to do extremely well in interviews, whereas candidates who understand only *what* to do generally are weeded out early in the process.

The book is organized into nine chapters that focus on (1) job market dynamics, (2) the structure of the financial world, (3) financial concepts that are important in company valuation, and (4) suggested readings. Highlighted in the text are various quotes from people in the financial services industry who have been active participants in the hiring process. Those quotes should provide insight from the other side of the hiring process. Finally, although this book deals with how to get a job on Wall Street, readers should take the term "Wall Street" as a broad reference to the entire financial services industry.

CHAPTER 1

GETTING THE JOB

Successful candidates understand what a bank is looking for. They prepare for interviews on a daily basis, beginning well beforehand, so that they can build a base of knowledge on which to draw. In doing this, they prepare a résumé that highlights what they have to offer a bank. Finally, they use the interview to strengthen their case rather than weaken it. In this chapter, we cover three areas. First, we discuss the qualities and characteristics a bank looks for in candidates. Second, we discuss the importance of the résumé along with a few basic pieces of advice. Third, we discuss the dos and don'ts of the interview itself.

AREAS OF FINANCE

The finance world typically is divided into the **buy side** and the **sell side**, terms that describe those who are tasked with buying securities on behalf of themselves or others and those who are tasked with selling securities on behalf of themselves or others. The sell side consists largely of units within the major investment banks (e.g., Goldman Sachs, JPMorgan), middle market investment banks (e.g., Harris Williams, Lincoln International), and smaller boutiques that tend to specialize (e.g., Howard Weil, which specializes in energy services). The buy side also includes units within the major investment banks but in addition covers mutual funds, private equity funds, and hedge funds. Commercial banks are also major players, acting as intermediaries between those who wish to save money and those who wish to invest those savers' money. In recent years, several major investment banks have joined forces with commercial banks to create much-needed balance sheet stability. For example, Bank of America and Merrill Lynch merged in late 2008 to form a massive organization with over $2 trillion in assets. In Chapter 4, we will return to this topic by discussing the different types of financial services firms.

HIERARCHY OF A BANK

The hierarchy of a financial services firm can differ from sector to sector and firm to firm but is relatively consistent in investment banks. Generally speaking, there are five levels in banks: analysts, associates, vice presidents, directors, and managing directors. *Analysts* are the entry-level analytical force of the firm. As entry-level workers, they are responsible for anything their superiors deem appropriate. They typically work more hours than their superiors, with those in investment banking sometimes being asked to work 16-plus hours per day for extended periods. Although most analysts leave the bank after two or three years, the very best of the analyst class are asked to stay at the firm and be promoted to associates. In addition, banks often hire students directly from MBA programs into associate positions. *Associates* are senior analysts who organize the work of analysts and assign tasks to members of the team. After a few years of successful work as an associate, an employee may be promoted to vice president. The work of *vice presidents* differs in a significant way from those who work under them because it is at the vice presidential level that interactions with clients become more extensive and more meaningful. Although vice presidents are responsible for managing the associates and analysts, they also interact with clients and potential clients on a regular basis. Put differently, vice presidents are somewhat of a hybrid between the analysts and associates who do the analytical work and the directors who generate business through their interactions with clients. Promotion from vice president to director is often difficult to achieve because there are few directors in relation to the number of vice presidents. In contrast to vice presidents, *directors* generally are not involved in the analytical process but instead concentrate almost solely on client interactions. Successful directors truly understand the financial world and are highly effective communicators. Furthermore, they have a commanding knowledge of the different tools firms use to achieve their goals. *Managing directors* represent the pinnacle of the company in the sense that a managing director is responsible for a bank's entire business within an area such as leveraged finance. They organize the efforts of the directors and work extensively with the executives of major companies in an effort to understand their needs and provide for them. As one might expect, directors and managing directors typically earn substantial salaries.

THE EASIEST PATH

Although there are many diverse paths that lead to Wall Street, the easiest path starts with an internship during the summer before a candidate's senior year in college. In recent years, banks have moved toward a model in which their entire full-time employee classes are selected from the pools of summer interns. Before this movement, banks would recruit a significant number of full-time, entry-level employees during the fall of their senior years in college. After that hiring period, the banks would turn their attention to juniors in an effort to hire them as interns for the following summer. This effectively meant that the banks would go through two back-to-back recruiting seasons. Because bankers play a very active role in the recruiting process, this structure necessarily meant that bankers spent a great deal of time on activities that generated no direct income for the firm. As a result, the major banks have opted to move to a single internship recruiting season, all but eliminating the traditional recruiting of fall-term seniors. As in any business, of course, there can be exceptions when unexpected needs arise.

> In hiring interns and analysts (into what is typically a two- to three-year program), we look for (1) genuine interest and curiosity in the job, (2) intellect and analytical skills, and (3) teamwork. In hiring associates (which we generally view as more permanent hires), we look beyond just those three characteristics. Is the candidate a self-starter? Will the candidate make a good long-term partner? Basically, we want to see leadership skills and an ability to interface with clients.
> —John Church
> Managing Director and Group Head
> Industrials Investment Banking, Wells Fargo

Because the recruiting of college juniors has increased in importance, banks increasingly are looking for juniors who worked in finance during the summer after their sophomore year. Ironically, however, many banks shy away from hiring sophomore interns because they fear those interns will want to try something different the next summer. To combat this, some major banks are seeking to hire sophomore interns into their satellite offices and then move them to New York for their junior internship experience. The hope is that this change of scenery will be enough to keep a candidate in the fold and therefore give the bank a clear advantage in its effort to hire the best interns into full-time positions.

Some firms have become quite creative in their recruiting strategies. For example, Harris Williams, which is perhaps the premier middle-market investment bank in the world, recently eliminated the typical summer internship experience in favor of something it believes is much better for both the candidate and the firm. To understand why the firm made that decision, note that a typical deal at Harris Williams takes about six months to complete. Because a summer internship is at most a three-month experience, the firm found that it could not provide its interns with more than a partial deal experience. To address this deficiency, the firm opted to create a boot camp of sorts in which candidates experience an entire deal in a compressed two-week time frame. In contrast to firms that carefully guard their top prospects, Harris Williams does not hire the boot camp students for the entire summer but instead encourages them to work elsewhere for the rest of the season. The firm believes that the two-week experience gives the candidates a real feel for what working at the firm would be like. The firm also believes that it will be able to compete successfully to hire those candidates into full-time jobs. Although the Harris Williams boot camp model is only a few years old, early numbers indicate that the firm has been quite successful in retaining candidates even if they work at other firms after the boot camp.

The main lesson from considering the current internship structure is that students who want to work in finance should focus on getting some sort of finance-related experience in the summer after their sophomore year and should use that experience as a launching pad to get a junior experience/internship at the firm they ultimately would like to work for as a full-time employee after graduation. Although it is not impossible to get to Wall Street without those summer experiences, it is becoming increasingly difficult.

THE JOB PROCESS

The job process in finance can vary widely across the different financial sectors, but the major investment banks all have a similar framework. With that in mind, we will continue to focus on the investment banks while recognizing that recruiting for other sectors may vary a bit. Furthermore, we will focus on the recruiting of undergraduate students but will spend some time discussing how the recruiting of more senior candidates differs. From the broadest perspective, the process can be broken down into five segments:

1. Networking with current and former Wall Street employees
2. Submission of an application (including a cover letter and résumé)
3. Phone and/or on-campus interviews
4. Super Days
5. Offers

Networking

No matter how qualified the candidate or how polished the résumé, a candidate has no chance to get the job unless that résumé gets into the hands of someone with the power to hire. Students and graduates of some universities have a clear advantage here because there is a great deal of academic nepotism on Wall Street: Harvard graduates prefer to hire other Harvard graduates, Wharton graduates prefer to hire other Wharton graduates, and so on. Furthermore, most banks create an annual list of **core schools** that they target in their hiring. Essentially, this means that the bank will devote financial resources to recruit students from those schools. Recruiting teams are formed within the bank, and those teams are tasked with identifying and recruiting the best students at those schools. Often, this means that members of the recruiting team will make multiple visits to campus during the school year to engage students and eventually interview them on campus. The engagement typically consists of information sessions in which the recruiting team educates students about the job and the job process and has dinners with select groups of students.

> The key is finding a connection . . . any connection. . . . Find existing alumni or friends of friends at the firm and reach out to them. . . . There rarely is a better advocate internally when you are essentially starting from "zero.". . . Without making a connection you are at a severe disadvantage by applying through the general pool. . . .
>
> —Keith Pelt
> Managing Director, Global Consumer Group
> Deutsche Bank

Although there are clear advantages to being a student at or having attended a core school, students from other schools should not be discouraged. There is so much pressure to perform that if one candidate clearly outshines the others, the job nearly always goes to the best candidate regardless of academic pedigree. The trick is of course to be considered in the first place. For students from noncore schools, the single best approach is to network. That is, the candidate identifies fellow alumni, friends, or family members who are employed on Wall Street and contacts them in hopes they will make a case within the firm for hiring the candidate. A university typically has both an alumni office and a career services office, either of which should be able to help a candidate identify alumni working on Wall Street. For the purposes of our discussion, we will refer to one of these Wall Street employees (alumni, friend, or family) as a *contact*. Networking is a bit more difficult than it may seem because employees must be careful to protect their reputations within the firm. Wall Street can become very cutthroat during lulls in business activities, and employees who have hired poor performers often find themselves out of a job along with the poor performers. This means that the candidate will need to convince the contact that he or she will not disappoint if hired.

How does a candidate best network? It might seem that the candidate should just send an e-mail with a résumé attached and ask the contact for help in getting the job, but this is a rather presumptuous approach. If the contact is to provide significant help, the contact has to want to help the candidate. It follows that the candidate's first objective should be to get to know the contact as well as possible. There are a variety of ways to achieve this, but the candidate should plan to have several conversations with the contact before specifically asking for help. The contact may very well offer to help during the first conversation or two, but the candidate should not force the issue too early. Ideally, the candidate will make a trip to New York or wherever the target firm is located to meet with a contact or two at that firm. Of course this may not be practical for everyone.

Students often ask for a specific plan detailing how to network. It is difficult to structure this approach into a recipe for a candidate to follow in every situation, but a rough outline of a possible strategy follows:

1. E-mail the contact and ask to set up a time for a brief phone call to seek advice on getting a job at the firm.

2. During the phone call, ask for advice on the best way to get a job at the firm or elsewhere in the industry. Before concluding the phone call, ask the contact for permission to send a résumé to him or her for review.

3. When sending the résumé (via e-mail), let the contact know that you will call in a few days to get his or her reaction.

4. During the subsequent phone call, take careful notes on the contact's recommendations.

5. After the phone call, change the résumé to reflect the contact's recommendations. This may mean that you will end up with a different résumé for each firm, but it is better to heed the advice of each contact than to risk offending one of them.

6. Send the revised résumé back to the contact, specifically asking if your changes are consistent with his or her recommendations. If so, this may be the best time to ask if the contact would be willing to help guide you through the submission process. In many cases, this means that the contact will literally walk your résumé from door to door within the firm to make the case for interviewing you.

7. If at all possible during this process, ask to meet in person with the contact over coffee. Nothing expresses a desire for the job better than the candidate spending the time and money to travel to meet with the contacts.

Although the process just outlined may seem a bit trite, a surprisingly large number of candidates hurt their chances by rushing the networking process.

It is worth spending a few moments to address the possibility that the contact will not respond to the candidate's initial overtures. More often than not, that will be the case. After all, the contact may be working 80 to 100 hours a week in a frantic effort to land a major deal. The candidate should not be offended by the lack of response but should view it as a challenge. Wall Street places a high value on determination and aggressiveness, and so the candidate should make repeated efforts, including both e-mails and phone calls, before giving up on a contact. Furthermore, it is common for Wall Street employees to screen a potential candidate (either intentionally or unintentionally) by not responding to the initial overture. If the candidate does not want the job enough to try three or four times, the firm probably would not want to hire the candidate anyway.

The Application

An application is nothing more than a résumé with an accompanying cover letter. For students at core schools, applications often go directly to the recruiting team for review rather than being included in the overall pool of applications. This is a rather significant advantage. For students at noncore schools, applications typically must be submitted through an online site. Unfortunately, the odds can be quite long for those applicants, with the offer rate often being less than 1 percent at the major banks. More than anything, this points to the importance of networking so that the candidate has people on the inside who will work on his or her behalf.

Phone, Video, and/or Campus Interviews

For students at core schools, the first round of interviews typically is conducted on campus, where the recruiting team can interview a large number of candidates in a short time. For students at noncore schools, phone interviews or remote video interviews (via Skype, for example) are the norm for the first round. For the most part, the first interview is designed to get a feel for the candidate's personality and understanding of basic finance. Personality matters far more than most people realize, with highly qualified high grade point average (GPA) students often being passed over in favor of a candidate with a lower GPA who probably would be easy to work with. Candidates should not be afraid to show a sense of humor and by all means should smile at times during the interview. Knowledge of technical financial details is tested at subsequent interviews, and so candidates who are preparing for a first round interview should focus more on brushing up on current events and basic finance concepts and less on the technical details of financial analysis.

Super Days

Although internship offers sometimes are given out after the first interview, a more common approach is to invite the candidate to visit the firm on what is called a "super day." The super day is nothing more than a day on which the firm brings in a typically large number of candidates for a series of one-on-one interviews with employees of the firm. These days can be highly stressful because the candidate might have a half dozen interviews or so, with the interviewers often varying greatly in disposition and the content of the interviews varying greatly in difficulty. Some firms are highly organized in their approach, assigning each interview team the task of exploring a particular area with the candidate.

> We do look for some themes in interviewing candidates and then put together several interview teams. Each interview team will interview within the context of one of those themes.
>
> —Hiter Harris
> Cofounder and Managing Director
> Harris Williams

Although for the most part interviewers are cordial, there are certainly exceptions to this rule. Several years ago, a student reported back to me that when he entered the interviewer's office, the interviewer was reading the *Wall Street Journal* and did not acknowledge him in any way. After a minute or two of awkward silence, the student wisely interrupted to explain why the interviewer should give him an opportunity to make a case for the job. I do not know whether the interviewer was being rude or was strategically testing whether the student would be aggressive enough to interrupt, but the point is that students should expect the unusual on super days.

Offers

Job offers typically are extended within a few days of the super day but sometimes are made right away. For example, one of my former students was in the elevator leaving the building after interviews when he received a phone call asking him to come back upstairs. When he did, the firm extended an offer on the spot. Occurrences like that tend to be rare, though, with firms taking quick action only when a candidate is extraordinarily gifted or has another offer that is about to expire.

A common question concerns what a candidate should do if he or she has one offer but is still under consideration at another firm that he or she prefers. Generally, firms want to have as much information as possible, and so the candidate should let the preferred firm know about the offer and its deadline. That achieves two things that may benefit the candidate. First, it gives the preferred firm the opportunity to respond in some manner before the offer expires. This helps avoid a situation in which the candidate might choose to turn down the offer in hopes of getting one from the preferred firm, only to be left without a job when the preferred firm does not extend an offer. Second, the preferred firm receives a bit of confirmation that the candidate is indeed worthy. Wall Street firms are extremely competitive, and so news of another offer often prompts a firm to extend one right away. This competition exists throughout the process. Recently, a managing director of one of the major investment banks called me to discuss a visit to Washington and Lee University, where I teach. When I asked him when he would like to come to campus to interview our students, he responded, "One day before Goldman Sachs comes." Although there are few opportunities for candidates to take direct advantage of this sort of competition among the banks, sharing the news of an offer represents a significant opportunity for the candidate.

Another common question is whether offers are negotiable. The answer of course depends on the specific circumstance. It is fair to say that offers for senior positions are fully negotiable but it is somewhat risky to try to negotiate after receiving an offer for an entry-level position. The best approach seems to be to view the offer as a take-it-or-leave-it proposition. Candidates can negotiate minor details such as a start date, but the time to negotiate major details such as salary is after one has worked for the firm for a while and demonstrated clear value to the firm.

> The best advice I could offer anyone involved in a negotiation of any kind are these words from Thomas Jefferson: "Nothing gives one person so much advantage over another as to remain always cool and unruffled under all circumstances."
>
> —Matthew Bevin
> Founder and Principal
> Integrity Asset Management

Ethics in the Job Market

Because of the competitive nature of the financial world and a job candidate's desire to get the best job, ethical considerations often come into play. Most often, this happens when a bank extends an offer to a candidate. The National Association of Colleges and Employers (NACE) provides guidelines on job offers. Those guidelines state that employers should provide students with a minimum of three weeks to decide on an offer and should not compel students to make a decision earlier than six months before graduation. In addition, the guidelines state that employers should give students the opportunity to extend the offer period for a reasonable time to investigate other opportunities. Although most banks at least respect the spirit of these guidelines, there are exceptions. For example, I know of specific situations in which candidates have been asked to accept or reject a job offer on the spot, with the employer literally saying that the candidate had to respond before the end of the phone conversation. Although these **exploding offer** situations are rare and one reasonably can conclude that those employers might not provide the best employment opportunity, candidates should be prepared to be placed in an awkward situation when receiving an offer. In addition, candidates should be aware that they can and should push back in such situations in an effort to buy time.

In other situations, employers have been a bit crafty in making offers. For example, in a recent situation a candidate was called and asked how he would respond if he was given an offer. He then was given an offer only after he stated categorically that he would accept the offer if it was given. In this way, the employer manipulated the situation in such a way that the candidate felt compelled to respond on the spot. As with the exploding offer described in the previous paragraph, students should think in advance about how they want to respond if they are pressured to accept a job on very short notice.

In other rare situations, firms have rescinded offers when the expectation of future business weakened. This, of course, leaves the candidate without a job at a time when jobs are scarce. This "profits before people" mentality, although not pervasive across Wall Street, is at best unfortunate and at worst highly unethical. In addition, firms typically want candidates to commit for a two-year period, but the investment banks in particular often have laid off workers (in bad economic times) before the two years have been completed.

On the other side of the offer, candidates have been known to engage in questionable behavior. For example, a candidate might choose to continue interviewing with a firm after accepting a job at another firm. Although this may seem reasonable to some, it not only is considered unethical but also often results in candidates starting off their careers with a bad reputation. Although a large number of people work on Wall Street, the community is surprisingly closely knit, and candidates should be aware that word can spread very rapidly across the Street.

It may seem trite to say it, but integrity matters. Never compromise integrity. Never. If you do it even once, your reputation will precede you in ways that are not beneficial to your career. Regardless of your line of business, but certainly as it relates to the investment business, relationships are built on trust. The cornerstone of trust is integrity.

—Matthew Bevin
Founder and Principal
Integrity Asset Management

Some candidates seem to view the process as a game of sorts in which the winner is the person who gets the most offers. These candidates often extend the interview process as long as possible even though they already have decided which offer to accept. This may be the most unethical of the behaviors typically seen in this process. It not only misleads the firms but also often prevents friends or fellow students from getting an offer. For all but the very top few schools, schools may be allocated a specific num ber of slots for initial offers. When the process is dragged out, the school is disadvantaged because when the offer eventually is declined, it may be too late for the firm to make another offer to someone at that school. Furthermore, candidates are naive if they believe that this activity will not hurt their reputation. This raises the question of how anyone on Wall Street would find out about this type of behavior. Entry-level offers are rather boiler-plate, with all the major firms typically offering the same base salary and similar benefits packages. Suppose, then, that a candidate receives an offer from Goldman Sachs but delays accepting until he or she can obtain an offer from Morgan Stanley. When the candidate subsequently turns down Morgan Stanley in favor of Goldman, it is easy to infer that the candidate was shopping for offers to inflate his or her ego. That may be an incorrect inference in some cases, but candidates should be aware of that perception and act accordingly. Generally speaking, a candidate should delay accepting an offer only because he or she is seeking an offer at a clearly preferred firm.

The Market for Experienced Candidates
▼

Although firms look for many of the same characteristics in experienced candidates that they look for in undergraduates, the process is decidedly different. In particular, the market for undergraduates tends to be very structured whereas the market for those who have been out a few years tends to be individual-specific. There is typically no formal outreach program for senior candidates. Rather, candidates are identified through head-hunters or personal contacts. Headhunters play an important role on Wall Street because they help match firms with candidates who otherwise might have gone undetected. Because most

For more senior positions, employers look for (1) *achievement versus potential* (what candidates did in school is much less important than what they have done in the business world), (2) *expertise* (employers want to see focus), (3) *results* (employers want to see how candidates can add to ROI [return on investment] and growth and how they have accomplished goals in the real world), (4) *skills* (employers don't have time to train more senior employees, so they prefer candidates who worked at places that provided a great business education), (5) *leadership and ability to manage others* (candidates should point to times in their careers when they have led teams), and (6) *partnership* (employers are looking to make a longer-term hire and want to find candidates who will be good long-term partners).

—Nick Sayers
Vice President
Concentric Equity Partners

employees leave their initial employers after two to three years, headhunters tend to be very active in seeking out bankers who have been out of undergraduate school for one or two years. They contact the bankers in hopes of finding employment for them elsewhere. In return, the headhunters are compensated by the firms that engage them.

Although many candidates are identified by headhunters, many other candidates find new employment by networking. With this in mind, young investment bank employees should cultivate relationships with professional contacts carefully because those contacts will become good leads for job openings. In addition, these young employees should take leadership roles whenever possible and try to work on projects that will showcase them well when they interview for more senior positions.

> In hiring MBAs, we look for the same characteristics that we look for in undergraduates, but also require three years of solid work experience. That experience need not be in business or finance, but it must be a meaningful experience.
>
> —Robert Sadler, Jr.
> Former President and Chairman
> M&T Bank

In attempting to hire experienced candidates, firms often look beyond the financial services field. For example, an investment bank looking to hire someone to be part of a natural resources team might look to hire an engineer who worked in the oil and gas industry. Having specific expertise in a field is often more valuable than having experience working in finance. After all, the bank can easily teach an intelligent person how to do a reasonable financial analysis but cannot easily teach someone to understand the technology of a particular field.

> Top-tier hedge funds hire the majority of their analysts from invest-
> ment banking programs and sell-side positions within invest-
> ment banks. Some hedge funds prefer to hire junior bankers who
> have basic financial training and develop them internally, while
> others prefer to hire analysts with more experience and sector-
> specific knowledge.
>
> —Senior analyst at a well-known hedge fund,
> former bulge bracket investment banker (because of con-
> straints at his workplace, he cannot be quoted by name)

Perhaps the most common field that banks look to is accounting because experienced accountants have the in-depth knowledge of financial statements that banks desire. Because of this, entry-level candidates who are unsure whether they should work in accounting or finance are in most cases better off taking an accounting job to begin their careers. Accounting jobs tend to be more structured with more predictable work hours, yet at the same time they can offer an education that will be highly valued on Wall Street when firms look to hire more senior candidates.

> Transitioning from public accounting to investment banking can be a
> natural career progression. The ability to work within a client service
> model translates very well, and a strong accounting background is a
> major plus for the work of a finance analyst.
>
> —Michael Stefan
> Vice President of Global Corporate and Investment Banking
> Bank of America Merrill Lynch

CHAPTER 2

WHAT THE FIRM
IS LOOKING FOR

Although there are different ways to character-ize what a financial services firm wants to see in a candidate, the desired qualities fit into six basic categories: (1) personality, (2) understanding of and passion for the job, (3) raw intelligence and the ability to think on one's feet, (4) knowledge about current financial events, (5) knowledge about the firm itself, and (6) knowledge about basic finance. We will discuss each of these categories in basic terms in this chapter and discuss several of them in more detail later in the book.

PERSONALITY AND THE ABILITY TO WORK WITH OTHERS

Investment banking often involves long hours with an occasional all-nighter. As a result, the ability to get along well with others when under stress is not just a trait desired by banks but a requirement. Some bankers refer to the Tokyo Test, which is the idea that they do not want to hire anyone they would not like to sit next to on a long flight to Tokyo. What sort of person would you be interested in sitting beside, in close quarters, for half a day? It is someone who is not self-centered, who has a good but not offensive sense of humor, who is intellectually curious with enough knowledge to support a stimulating conversation, and who is polite with good hygiene. Hygiene should go without saying, but stories abound of candidates showing up for interviews smelling bad, having not showered or brushed their teeth that morning. Needless to say, those students do not get job offers. Interviewers pay careful attention to the appearance of a candidate because bankers often interact with clients. Appearing disheveled, slouching in the chair, making little eye contact, never smiling, and dressing poorly are all ways to not get the job regardless of the strength of the rest of a candidate's case.

> We are always interested in candidates who fit with our culture and can add value. Given our emphasis on finding the "right" people, we devote significant time and effort to our hiring process. At its core, the focus is to really understand the candidate: what are his or her strengths and areas of genius, what kind of potential does he or she have to grow, what are his or her ideal working conditions, etc., and does that match our needs. We're really just trying to determine whether we can develop a relationship that's mutually beneficial to both employer and employee.
>
> —Samantha McLemore
> Co-fund Manager,
> Legg Mason Capital Management Opportunity Trust
> Legg Mason Capital Management

In the days or weeks leading up to first-round interviews, some banks hold information sessions on campus or host dinners with candidates in an effort to get to know the candidates better. The successful candidates are the ones who are engaged at these gatherings but do not dominate them. They are not afraid to inject humor or tell a story about themselves, but they keep it short and relevant to the conversation. To evaluate personality during interviews, interviewers often engage the candidate on issues unrelated to the job, such as sports, travel, and world events. This presents a great opportunity for a candidate to change the nature of the interview from an "ask and answer questions" format to a real conversation. Generally speaking, the more conversational the tone of the interview, the better a candidate's chances of moving forward in the process.

> Some candidates are so well coached on the interviews that we sometimes try to look under the hood and find out what's in the soul of the candidate. . . . Sometimes how they express themselves is as important as what they say.
>
> —Hiter Harris
> Cofounder and Managing Director
> Harris Williams

Many firms feel so strongly about personality that it often represents the only "must-have" characteristic in candidates. For example, Bill Miller, who runs Legg Mason Capital Management and who famously beat the S&P 500 for 15 consecutive years, has said on more than one occasion that he will hire only "nice people." It goes beyond being nice, however. Recently, a student contacted me for advice about the finance job market. He was concerned because although he had a nearly perfect academic record, he was not competitive on the job market. The student had an always-happy sort of personality, and his peers seemed genuinely to like him. I talked to a few practitioners who had interviewed him and discovered that they believed his bubbly personality would "drive them crazy." Although in perhaps every other area candidates should strive to differentiate themselves, successful candidates tend to have personalities that do not unduly stand out from the crowd.

In hiring undergraduates, we look at top-tier schools primarily in the Northeast. Students must have a 3.5 minimum GPA and strong analytical skills. But how the students present themselves and how they communicate is also important, because they will need to deal with people at all levels of the organization. And they must have demonstrated leadership at school or outside of school as well. *Leadership is a big part.*

—Robert Sadler, Jr.
Former President and Chairman
M&T Bank

There are numerous ways for interviewers to explore personality. Questions typically are designed to get candidates to talk in narrative form about themselves.

SIQ1: *Tell me about yourself. Who are you?*

SIQ2: *What do you do in your spare time?*

SIQ3: *Tell me about a time you worked on a group project.*

Candidates should respond to these sorts of questions thoughtfully, taking every opportunity to connect the answers to the jobs they are seeking. For example, in answering SIQ1, the candidate might give a quick biography but in doing so be sure to highlight the events that led him or her to pursue a job in finance. The key thing to remember is that each answer should communicate something that makes the candidate seem like a good fit for the job. Furthermore, the candidate should only mention things that have some relevance to the job. Simply put, the candidate should answer questions along these lines with the expectation that the interviewer will follow up any response with a question such as "How does that make you more qualified for the job?"

UNDERSTANDING OF AND PASSION FOR THE JOB

Financial services jobs, particularly those in investment banking, can be difficult and trying, and so interviewers want to see evidence that a candidate knows what he or she is getting into. Therefore, it is important for a candidate to understand the typical organizational structure of an investment bank and have some idea of where he or she best fits into that structure. An important first step is for the candidate to demonstrate a working knowledge of the financial services world. To test this knowledge, interviewers often ask questions such as the following:

SIQ4: *Why are you interested in finance?*

SIQ5: *Where would you most like to work within the investment bank?*

SIQ6: *Where do you see yourself in 5 to 10 years?*

The candidate need not have an entire career path planned out or be able to draw the bank's organizational chart but at least should be able to name a few areas of interest within the bank and explain why he or she has those interests. The candidate also should be able to articulate what sort of career path he or she has in mind, even if it is only a "best guess at this time." Candidates should keep in mind that few investment bankers stay at the first job for more than a few years, and so it is okay to say something like "I'd like to work in banking for a few years, then go to business school, and then work in private equity."

Related to this is the idea that firms want to hire candidates who understand the commitment it takes to succeed on Wall Street. Those who do not have this understanding yet find

> For many interviewers, a critical issue when considering a lateral hire is understanding the reasons behind the candidate's career transition. It is important to have a coherent story, framing past decisions and experiences in light of your interests and how a career in investment banking fits that narrative.
>
> —Michael Stefan
> Vice President, Global Corporate and Investment Banking
> Bank of America Merrill Lynch

their way to Wall Street anyway tend to view their time there as something akin to a prison sentence. For those who remember the stress of taking final exams in college, life as an entry-level analyst is somewhat like having several final exams scheduled every single week for two years. Because of this, interviewers often devote a significant portion of their interviews to investigating whether candidates can tolerate that stress.

> I often find that many summer internship or full-time analyst candidates are misguided about what it takes to secure a job on Wall Street. Many are simply following the herd mentality. They either convince themselves or are told by friends or family that they have what it takes to make it. Few candidates truly ask themselves if they are, in fact, prepared to work on Wall Street and have the necessary qualifications, skills, and commitment to succeed in the role of analyst at a major investment bank. It is this group of introspective candidates that generally succeeds in the analyst role. This is a highly coveted quality!
>
> —Akshat Shah
> Director in Health Care Investment Banking
> UBS

Interviewers also try to assess whether the candidate really understands not only the job but the overall objective of the job. Often these questions sound simple, but they give candidates an opportunity to make a very strong and positive impression.

SIQ7: *What is* _____ *?*
(investment banking, commercial banking, etc.)

SIQ8: *How does the bank make money?*

SIQ7 is designed to test whether candidates understand what the firm does. We will address question SIQ8 in a more significant way later in the book, but for now simply note that financial services firms typically make money by providing advice to clients and/or by acting as an intermediary between the buyers of securities and the sellers of securities. In doing so, firms sell at a slightly higher price than the price at which they bought, pocketing the **spread** on the transactions.

RAW INTELLIGENCE AND THE ABILITY TO THINK ON ONE'S FEET

Most banks are open to hiring students who have little or no financial background. In fact, Wall Street is home to many nonbusiness majors such as those with English or mathematics degrees. For example, the CEOs of several of the world's largest banks majored in nontraditional fields. Brian Moynihan (Bank of America), John Mack (Morgan Stanley), and Lloyd Blankfein (Goldman Sachs) majored in history (at Brown, Duke, and Harvard, respectively). Vikram Pandit (Citigroup) majored in engineering at Gannon University. Oswald Grübel (Group CEO at UBS AG) did not attend university at all. The banks believe that they can teach any intelligent and curious person how to be a successful financial analyst, and so it is sufficient if a candidate works well with others and truly wants to work on Wall Street. Still, the candidate's academic record is an important indicator of intelligence and the ability to complete work successfully in a timely fashion.

We look for smart, high-potential candidates who are good cultural fits. We obviously look for all the standard stuff: good GPA, evidence of broad interests/activities, desire to be in the business, etc. But we think cultural fit is critically important. Our values emphasize excellence, thought leadership, intellectual curiosity, and adaptability, among other things. We also highly prioritize respect, kindness, and teamwork. The work environment at LMCM differs greatly from other cultures where individuals more directly compete with peers for advancement and development opportunities. Different people thrive under different conditions. To optimize hiring decisions, the working environment should suit the individual's natural style.

—Samantha McLemore
Co-fund Manager, Legg Mason Opportunity Trust
Legg Mason Capital Management

Although interviewers can learn a lot about a candidate's intelligence from a well-crafted résumé, they sometimes put candidates on the spot by asking difficult or seemingly impossible questions.

SIQ9: *How many Ping-Pong balls will fit in a bus?*

SIQ10: *What is the angle between the hour hand and the minute hand of a clock at one-thirty?*

Although such questions may seem absurd, there is a point to them. Analysts often are faced with seemingly difficult or impossible tasks, and so it is important for the interviewer to get a feel for how well a candidate will deal with those situations. Successful candidates are the ones who respond to questions like SIQ9 by thinking through a process by which the answer can be estimated. Candidates should not be afraid to think out loud but should spend a moment or two silently thinking before explaining their logic. For questions like SIQ10, which is a common sales and trading question, the interviewer is looking to see if the candidate can come up with the precise answer. It is helpful in that situation for the candidate to think out loud as he or she computes the answer. That way, if the candidate makes a silly math error but has the basic intuition right, the interviewer will go away with a positive impression of the candidate. Consider, for example, the following possible responses to SIQ9.

Response 1: "I don't know, but I'd say it's about 10,000."

Response 2: "Well, we could estimate the number in three steps. First, we compute the volume of the bus and make adjustments for features such as the seats, which take up space. Second, we estimate the number of balls that would fit into some smaller yet manageable volume. For example, we could see how many balls fit into a box. That effectively gives us the density of the balls. Third, we multiply the volume of the bus by that estimated density to get an estimate for the entire bus."

It is clear that Response 1 does nothing to help the candidate's case. It tells the interviewer nothing about how the candidate thinks. It also gives the interviewer the impression that the candidate is not intellectually curious. After all, a curious person presented with that question surely would at least pause to think about how to come up with a reasonable estimate. Perhaps more important, Response 1 suggests that the candidate might tend to take shortcuts in an analysis. Rather than take the time to develop a reasonable estimate, the candidate might rely on his or her instincts. Although confidence is certainly a desired trait on Wall Street, the firm cannot run the risk that such confidence will bias a financial analysis.

> The most demanding part of being an equity sales trader is prioritizing your tasks. You may receive an order from a customer, and before you have time to enter it, the phone rings and you have to answer it. Simultaneously, a trader is yelling a bunch of numbers at you and an analyst is talking over the squawk box about his latest report. All of this is going on while you have four screens of information in front of you. Multitasking, delivering under pressure, analyzing a situation quickly; these are all important traits to have on the trading floor.
>
> —John Jensen
> Vice President, International Equity Sales Trading
> Bank of America Merrill Lynch

Candidates for sales and trading positions often face questions dealing with mathematical calculations and expectations. After all, traders must be able to provide quotes on a security within a few seconds of a request. This requires that the trader be able to do simple math (addition, subtraction, multiplication, and division but generally nothing more advanced) very, very quickly without making an error. Furthermore, traders must be aware that it might be advantageous to lose money on an initial trade with a client in order to build a relationship and attract more business down the road. Thus, traders must understand the notion that the ideal objective is not to maximize the profit on a particular trade but to maximize the present value of the stream of profits generated through a particular client. Although the types of questions candidates are asked vary a great deal, a few questions have become somewhat common.

SIQ11: What is the square root of 2,000?

SIQ12: Suppose I give you a six-sided die and offer to give you a dollar times the number that you roll. Suppose also that I give you the option to reroll the die one time after observing the outcome of the initial roll. How much should I expect to have to pay you?

SIQ11 is designed as a simple test of how fast the candidate thinks when doing simple math calculations. Usually the number given is a multiple of 100, so the candidate can quickly factor out the 100 (which has a square root of 10) and then deal with what is left quickly. In this case, the square root of 2000 is 10 times the square root of 20, which in turn is 20 times the square root of 5.

SIQ12 is designed to test the candidate's understanding of expectations. In this question and others of its type, the key is for the candidate to work the problem backward by starting with the contingent second roll. The expected value on that roll is $3.50, and so the candidate should choose to redo the first roll if the die shows any value less than 3.5 (i.e., 1, 2, or 3). Thus, with probability 0.5 the candidate would reroll with the expectation on that second roll of $3.50 in value. With probability 0.5 the candidate would achieve a roll of 4, 5, or 6. This outcome has an expected value of 5, and so the overall expected value would be 0.5 × $3.50 + 0.5 × $5.00 = $4.25. Candidates should not feel too comfortable after answering SIQ12 correctly because it often is followed by a related question.

SIQ13: Okay, now that you have correctly answered $4.25, how does the expectation change if I allow you to reroll a second time if you wish?

As with SIQ12, the answer is easily computed by using backward induction. With one reroll permitted, the expectation is $4.25. Adding another potential reroll simply means that the initial decision is whether to accept the first roll or proceed to the game described in SIQ12. Since that has an expectation of $4.25, the roller would reroll after the first roll whenever the die shows a number less than 4.25 (i.e., 1, 2, 3, or 4). This occurs with probability $^2/_3$. A 5 or 6 will occur with probability $^1/_3$, and that event has an expected value of 5.5. It follows that the expected value of the game described in SIQ13 is $(^2/_3) \times \$4.25 + (^1/_3) \times \$5.50 = \$4.67$.

At this point, it is worth spending a few minutes to demonstrate that human beings tend to overestimate their own abilities. Employees who understand this basic idea are more likely to double-check their work, verify supposed facts, and make only claims that have strong support. To convince you that human beings overestimate their own abilities, consider the following set of 10 questions. Answer each question with a 90 percent confidence interval. That is, in answering each question provide a *range* of numbers such that you are 90 percent certain that the correct answer falls in that range. For example, suppose you are asked, "What is the diameter of the earth in kilometers?" You would not answer "0 to 100,000,000 kilometers" in an effort to be certain you are correct but would answer something like "7,000 to 8,000 kilometers" in an effort to try to be (as precisely as possible) 90 percent certain you will be right on that individual question.

1. What is the area of Canada in square miles?
2. When was George Washington born?
3. How far are we *in meters* from the nearest star other than our sun?
4. What is the height of Mount Everest in meters?
5. How deep is the deepest point in the oceans?

6. How many live births were recorded in the United States in 1943 (which is often designated as the beginning of the baby boom)?

7. What was the population of the United States as of January 1, 1960?

8. What was the level of the S&P 500 Index at the close of trading on December 31, 1985?

9. What is the distance between Paris, France, and Perth, Australia, measured as the crow flies?

10. What is the wingspan of the NASA's space shuttle?

Readers should answer each of these questions *before* taking a look at the answers, which are given at the end of this chapter. This sort of test is a popular component of more than a few books, including John Nofsinger's *The Psychology of Investing*. The test is a simple way to assess whether people have accurate perceptions of their own abilities. If they do, they should answer 9 of the 10 questions correctly on average. Although it is difficult to draw firm conclusions at the individual level by using such a small sample of questions, research has shown that people on average answer far fewer than nine questions correctly. After answering these questions, check them against the correct ones at the end of this chapter. Chances are that you will have correctly answered well below nine questions.

Being confident is not the same as being cocky. Prospective employees should remember their attitude is being questioned as much as their intelligence.

—John Jensen
Vice President, International Equity Sales Trading
Bank of America Merrill Lynch

What lesson do we learn from this exercise? Although there is no shortage of incredibly bright people on Wall Street, there is not that fine a line between those who are arrogant yet understand their own limitations and those who start off with the notion that their beliefs and instincts are better than everyone else's. Confidence is valued very highly on Wall Street, but arrogance generally is despised. Candidates should always remember the Tokyo Test and act accordingly. Few people would want to sit next to an arrogant person on a flight to Tokyo, but most people would have no problem sitting next to a confident person.

> Remember, there is a fine line between confidence and cockiness. . . . That said, without crossing that line, use the interview process to position yourself mentally inside the company as if you already have the job. Timidity and desperation do not serve job seekers well. Confidence, intellectual curiosity, and innovative thinking do.
>
> —Matthew Bevin
> Founder and Principal
> Integrity Asset Management

KNOWLEDGE OF FINANCIAL CURRENT EVENTS

Successful financial analysts are the ones who are in some way passionate about the job. As a result, firms want to hire those who at least track the financial world on a regular basis. This is more important than most candidates realize because a solid foundation in the real world is a critical part of interactions with clients. Imagine, for example, that a client asks a banker about a deal that was written up in the *Wall Street Journal* only to find that the banker has not heard about it. Would the client want to hire that banker? In the same way, would a bank want to hire a job candidate who might ruin a deal with a client by not being up to speed on current financial events?

A typical strategy for an interviewer is to ask the candidate what he or she reads and follow up by asking about specific articles the candidate has read or should have read.

SIQ14: *What financial publications do you read?*

To prepare for questions like these, the candidate should read the *Wall Street Journal* every day in the few weeks leading up to an interview. If the candidate does not have time to read every article completely, he or she should at least read the first and last paragraphs of every article. Those paragraphs will provide the important points of the story and give the candidate enough information to have an intelligent conversation about the topic. Ideally, the candidate will read a second publication (e.g., *The Economist, Barron's*) regularly to show depth of interest in the financial markets. It is perhaps unnecessary to say this, but candidates who exaggerate how much they read are quickly revealed as the interviewer asks questions about their reading.

A candidate also should follow the news reports on several major companies every day and should have read entirely through at least one company's most recent 10-K or 10-Q report.

SIQ15: *What companies have you been following lately?*

Some interviewers have been known to ask a candidate to name a company he or she has been following. After the candidate responds, the interviewer asks for another company and then another. After the candidate names a third or fourth company, the interviewer quizzes the candidate on that company. That sort of approach (there are others as well) allows the interviewer to test both the candidate's passion for finance and depth of investigation into the financial world.

KNOWLEDGE ABOUT THE FIRM

Financial services firms receive applications from hundreds if not thousands of candidates. Successful candidates are the ones who differentiate themselves by showing a clear effort to prepare for the interview and aggressively pursue the job. An important part of demonstrating this effort is the candidate's advance preparation for the interviews. After all, if a candidate does not care enough about his or her career to spend a few minutes preparing for interviews, the firm surely could not trust the candidate to put forth a solid effort on behalf of a client.

SIQ16: *Why do you want to work for us instead of another firm?*

SIQ17: *Why do you think you are a good fit for us?*

These questions are designed to give a candidate opportunities to talk about the firm. At the very least, while answering these questions, the candidate should throw in a few facts about the company and show that he or she spent some time reading up on it. Some interviewers are even more direct, asking questions like the following:

SIQ18: *What do you know about us?*

There are a few simple things a candidate can do to prepare for these questions.

1. Read the company's Web site carefully. Note major news items and recent deals. Attempt to figure out what the company believes is important. Get a sense for the culture of the company, the size and scope of operations, and evidence of the firm's success.

2. Read the company's profile on other Web sites (e.g., www.vault.com, finance.google.com).

3. Understand how the company makes money. Financial institutions act primarily as intermediaries. Generally speaking, they make money either by charging fees for services or by acting as a **market maker**. Fees might come from advising a firm on a merger or on any number of financing-related issues that firm might face. A *market maker* is simply an intermediary that buys assets at one price and then tries to sell them to others at higher prices, pocketing the difference.

KNOWLEDGE OF BASIC FINANCE

Surprisingly, basic financial knowledge is *not* an absolute requirement for the job. Still, it is a big plus if the candidate can demonstrate a solid understanding of finance basics. This is particularly important for business, accounting, and economics majors, who are expected to have that understanding. Candidates with majors in other fields are held to a lower standard on financial knowledge but a higher standard on demonstrating a true interest in finance. For example, a math major who has gone out of his or her way to learn basic finance outside the classroom is viewed very favorably by banks, more favorably in fact than a business major who has developed a solid but not spectacular knowledge of finance.

Interviewers tend to begin by asking relatively simple questions and go on to ask increasingly difficult questions to get a sense of the depth of the candidate's knowledge. Some interviewers keep raising the level of difficulty until the candidate admits to not knowing the answer. That allows the interviewer to get a feel for the extent of the candidate's knowledge. Opinions differ on how a candidate should respond if he or she does not know

I believe there are certain thresholds when looking at the numbers on the résumé. [The candidate should have] at least a 3.5 GPA (and if not overall, it should be at least that in the major) and high 600s on the math portion of the SAT. After that I look at majors (the candidate must have taken at least a few business classes that are applicable to the job), and if the major is not business-related, I expect the GPA to be proportionately higher. In other words, if [I am] comparing a philosophy to an accounting major where both have a 3.5 GPA, then I will give the interview to the business major every time. If, however, the philosophy major has a 3.9 GPA, I would be more willing to take a chance [on the philosophy major] than the accounting major with the 3.5 GPA.

—Keith Pelt
Managing Director, Global Consumer Group
Deutsche Bank

the answer to a question. Some interviewers prefer candidates who are entirely forthright about their knowledge, but recently one of my students was lambasted by an interviewer when the student said she did not know the answer to a question. The interviewer responded that you should always act like you know the answer even if you have no idea. Perhaps the best advice is to take the middle ground and provide a carefully hedged response in which you provide your best guess as an appropriate answer.

A typical first question in an interviewer's attempt to assess a candidate's financial knowledge is the following:

SIQ19: *Which is cheaper, debt or equity?*

Successful candidates are the ones who provide reasonable answers to these sorts of questions and then very briefly give the logic behind their answers. It is okay, for example, to say that "**debt** is cheaper than **equity**," but it is much better to say that "debt is cheaper than equity because it has a senior claim on firm assets, has tax-deductible payments. . . ." Generally, interviewers look for knowledge in four areas: (1) time value of money, (2) accounting, (3) **capital structure**, and (4) valuation. Seniors looking for full-time jobs of course are held to a higher standard than are juniors looking for internships. Similarly, business, accounting, and economics majors are held to a higher standard than are those with other majors. In any case, firms place a high value on a candidate's financial instincts.

> There are successful investors of many different styles. One similarity they all share is that investing is more than a job, it's a passion, it's a lifestyle. It's a very competitive business with very high economic rewards, so you're competing against people who are consumed with it. It's not a profession where you can phone it in. Other than that, I am reminded of a quote by champion poker player Puggy Pearson often referenced by Bill [Miller, chairman and chief investment officer of Legg Mason Capital Management] because of its applicability to investing. "Only three things to gamblin' (investing): knowing the 60/40 end of a proposition, money management, and knowing yourself." Basically, you need to understand when the odds are in your favor, make the appropriate-size bets, and know yourself (your instincts, your competitive advantage, your common mistakes, etc.). I think those are the keys.
>
> —Samantha McLemore
> Co-fund manager
> Legg Mason Capital Management Opportunity Trust
> Legg Mason Capital

In Chapters 5 and 6 we will discuss the basics of accounting and finance so that readers can understand the terminology and be able to articulate a few key concepts. At that time, we will revisit the debt-equity choice because it is at the very core of what investment banks do.

ABILITY TO SUSTAIN AN INTELLIGENT CONVERSATION

In trying to generate business, the deal pitch is obviously critical. What is not so obvious is that simple, seemingly innocuous conversations with potential clients can be just as important. Companies want to hire people who are intelligent and can think on their feet. In contrast to the interview, in which for the most part the interviewer is looking for candidates with a specific set of knowledge, conversations with potential clients can cover virtually any topic. Recognizing that a new hire might very well be on the phone with CEOs and chief financial officers (CFOs), some interviewers will throw out what might be termed wild card questions to see how well the candidate responds. Often these conversations occur when the candidate does not know he or she is being interviewed. For example, firms often hold information sessions on campuses or take groups of students out to a casual dinner. These meetings are cast as an opportunity for the candidate to learn more about the firm, but they also act as an initial round of interviewing. With that in mind, candidates should be ready to have an intelligent discussion of any topic that comes up. Although it is difficult to prepare for those conversations, there are a few things a candidate can do to build a foundation he or she can rely on. First, the candidate should have a solid understanding of what has gone on in the financial world and the macroeconomy over the last few decades, with special emphasis on more recent times. Chapter 8 of this book provides a commentary covering some of the key financial developments of the last decade. That discussion is not meant to be an exhaustive one but to provide a basic understanding of how various events have affected the financial world. Second, there is a growing body of literature that interviewers expect candidates to have read or at least be familiar with. Chapter 9 provides a list of books that candidates should begin reading. Although there are a few books that are must-reads, for the most part a candidate should start with the books that sound the most interesting. Doing so increases the likelihood that the candidate will retain information that will prove useful in an interview. Said differently, the type of book a candidate reads is less important than being able to demonstrate a habit of reading interesting books.

> Above all, they must be well rounded with multiple activities and good grades.
>
> —Keith Pelt
> Managing Director, Global Consumer Group
> Deutsche Bank

ABILITY TO GENERATE BUSINESS

Hiring in the financial services industry is divided roughly into two tiers: hiring of temporary employees and hiring of permanent employees. In the former tier are employees who are hired right out of undergraduate school to act as an analytical labor force. They develop valuation models, prepare pitch books, and generally do anything that might be needed to help the bank land a deal. These employees are viewed as being temporary in the sense that most of them stay with the firm for only two or three years, after which they typically leave to work at **buy side** firms or go to business school. In the other tier of hiring, banks typically hire students right out of business school or from other firms, expecting those hires to engage in work well beyond basic analytics. These employees are viewed as permanent hires in the sense that the bank's objective is to keep the best of them for their entire careers.

To this point in our discussion, we have discussed characteristics that are sought in every employee. For more senior candidates, firms look for an additional characteristic: the potential to develop new business for the firm. The natural extension of that idea is to ask what it is about some people that makes them naturally able to close deals. Although it is difficult to write down the specific elements of this ability, it is clear that to generate new business an individual must be a good leader and must be able to persuade potential clients. Interviewers can address these areas in a number of ways, but for candidates with prior banking experience, the interview often focuses on that prior experience.

SIQ20: *What successful deals have you worked on?*
What role did you play in those deals?

Successful candidates are the ones who are able to highlight times when they have gone beyond the call of duty to finish the job and times when they have assumed leadership roles on the deal team. Of course, candidates should be aware that Wall Street is a tightly knit community and that exaggerations or outright lies generally are revealed rather quickly.

SIQ21: *What have you built in the past?*

Although the question seems entirely open-ended, it presents an opportunity for candidates to draw parallels between their prior activities and the idea of building a business. The quality of an answer of course depends on those prior activities, but successful candidates tend to be those who are able to show a clear and structured approach to creating something noteworthy. Questions such as these are less about *what* the candidate has built and more about *how* the candidate built it.

For candidates without prior banking experience, the interviews often focus on prior work experience or the MBA experience.

> SIQ22: *What leadership positions did you assume while in graduate school?*

> SIQ23: *In your previous work experience, what roles did you play in group efforts?*

Although the clear advice here is for candidates to tailor their responses to show leadership strengths, the more subtle advice is for candidates to anticipate these sorts of questions in future interviews and do things now to create ammunition for those later interviews. For example, most schools have investment clubs. What better way is there to show leadership potential in the financial world than by taking a leadership role in an investment club? Furthermore, most of these clubs are based on the idea that students will analyze an investment and then present it to the larger group in an effort to persuade them to approve the recommended allocation.

> SIQ24: *What situations have you been in where you had to persuade others to adopt your point of view? How did you approach those situations?*

In answering questions like these, candidates should keep in mind that it is easiest to persuade others if the facts support the claims. It is easy to jump the gun and talk about the actual persuasive conversation, but a better approach is to talk first about how you prepared for that conversation. Banks want to hire candidates who thrive on being meticulous and well prepared, and so questions such as this one give candidates an additional opportunity to show those characteristics.

ANSWERS TO SELF-PERCEPTION TEST
(pages 34–35)

1. 3.854 million square miles (9.985 million square kilometers): from atlast.nrcan.gc.ca

2. February 22, 1732: from www.mountvernon.org

3. 38,000,000,000,000,000 meters (Proxima Centauri): from hyperphysics.phy-astr.gsu.edu

4. 29,035 feet (8,850 meters): from www.mountainzone.com

5. 35,840 feet (10,9724 meters): from www.geology.com

6. 2,934,860: from www.cdc.gov

7. 179,386,000: from research.stlouisfed.org

8. 211.28: from www.standardandpoors.com

9. 8,865 miles (14,276 kilometers): from www.travelmath.com

10. 78 feet (23.8 meters): from www.nasa.gov

CHAPTER 3

THE RÉSUMÉ AND INTERVIEWS

The résumé is a critical part of getting a job because it represents the candidate's best chance to get the initial interview. There are a few rules that students should follow in preparing a résumé:

1. For undergraduate candidates, the résumé should include the cumulative GPA to the hundredths decimal place, and candidates should make sure it is accurate. Reviewers will assume that GPAs such as 3.4 are either estimates or rounded numbers, and so such GPAs generally are viewed as being untrustworthy. A major GPA is not required but should be included if it does not hurt the candidate's case.

2. With one exception, the résumé should include only activities that demonstrate skills or qualities that are directly applicable to the job. The exception is that candidates should fill in any time gaps in the résumé wherever possible. Employers generally do not like to see periods of unproductive time on a candidate's résumé. Therefore, a candidate should list a summer job even if the job does not seem specifically relevant to the financial services industry. Although juniors to a certain extent can get away with having taken a lazy summer after their sophomore year, it is far

better if they can show some sort of productive activity. Seniors, in contrast, will be penalized significantly if they did not spend the summer after their junior year doing something productive. Furthermore, candidates who did finance-related work during that summer are viewed far more favorably than are candidates who did not.

3. The résumé should include only those items for which the candidate can articulate clearly why they were put on the résumé. Key themes include but are not limited to showing discipline, showing leadership, showing work ethic, and showing finance experience.

4. *Do not exaggerate.* It is critical that the candidate's interview strengthen his or her case rather than weaken it. Significant exaggerations, which are almost always discovered by good interviewers, have the opposite effect because the candidate appears weaker in the interview than on paper and potentially even appears untrustworthy. The reality is that if a candidate has to exaggerate to get the job, he or she is probably not qualified enough to be successful at it. In investment banking, this leads to a rather miserable experience with a quick exit from the finance world.

The candidate should view the résumé as a preemptive attempt to control the interview. Every line on the résumé is important because it is an invitation for the interviewer to ask questions. With that in mind, the résumé should provide enough information to cover the basic facts but not so much that it leaves the interviewer with no questions to ask. The résumé should make the reader want to know more about the items that best highlight the candidate's qualifications for the job. One recent internship candidate had started a credit union in high school. By placing only a brief note about that on the résumé, she left reviewers wanting to know more. This meant that a portion of

I typically like to see a résumé where the candidate has excelled and developed adaptable skills from a previous employment, demonstrates outstanding academic and extracurricular achievement, possesses strong analytical and quantitative skills, and is enthusiastic about, committed to, and hungry to succeed in investment banking. The candidate should display an ability to work in a team environment. Lastly, and I cannot stress this enough, interpersonal skills is a highly valued commodity. Given the high-stress environment, you want to be around nice, cordial people who are pleasant and lighten the mood.

—Akshat Shah
Director in Health Care Investment Banking
UBS

her interviews was devoted to a topic of her choosing rather than the interviewer's.

Each part of the interview fits into one of three categories: answering questions, asking questions, and having a conversation. Answering questions is certainly the most critical part, but the other areas should not be discounted. It is difficult to prepare for a general conversation, and so we will focus on answering and asking questions.

A candidate can make a variety of mistakes in answering questions. Some candidates talk too much and go beyond what the interviewer has asked about. Others give very short correct answers but do not take the next step to justify their answers briefly. Others give memorized answers that, although correct, tell the interviewer nothing more than that the candidate is capable of memorization. Other candidates respond too quickly without carefully thinking through their answers. Others repeatedly pause during their answers, filling the gaps with "ums" and "uhs." Still others honestly answer "I don't know" to some questions but pass up the opportunity to say what they do know. With all this in mind, successful candidates are ones who

1. Are not afraid of silence. They pause to consider how to answer a question before starting to speak. They do not fill gaps with "ums" and "uhs" but let silence give the impression of deep thought.
2. Do not memorize answers but instead concentrate on saying what they know in their own words.
3. Are not afraid to admit a lack of knowledge in some area but always follow by offering what they do know or explaining how they would go about finding the answer.

Each question is an opportunity for the candidate to reveal something positive. Successful candidates seize those opportunities to support claims they have made about themselves or claims they want to make.

In most interviews, the interviewer will reserve a few minutes at the end of the scheduled time so that the candidate has a chance to ask questions. It is easy for the candidate to relax at this point, thinking that the interview is essentially over. That is not the case because the opportunity to ask questions is also an opportunity to strengthen the candidate's case. Furthermore, by not asking questions the candidate not only leaves the impression of a lack of intellectual curiosity but misses an opportunity to let the interviewer see the specific nature of that curiosity.

SIQ25: *What questions do you have for me?*

Some interviewers feel so strongly about SIQ25 that candidates who ask no questions or ask canned ones are eliminated from consideration even if the rest of the interview went well. What makes a question a good one to ask? In my experience, candidates who are preparing for interviews often go around asking other people for their advice about good questions to ask. Although this seems like a reasonable part of preparing for an interview, it largely misses the point. A question is a good one if it is relevant to the discussion and if the candidate is truly curious about it. Prepared or memorized questions are better than nothing, but they generally leave the interviewer with the impression that the candidate is not excited about the job. After all, there is no way a candidate can know everything about the job and no way a candidate can be excited about the job and not be curious.

There are some limitations on questions, of course. For example, asking about salaries or vacation time early in the process probably hurts rather than helps. Still, the best approach is simply to ask about what you want to know. If you want to know what percentage of interns typically receive full-time offers at the end of the summer, ask about it. If you don't understand how the internship experience works, ask about it. This is also a chance to develop a slightly more personal connection with the interviewer by asking about his or her experiences on the job. Generally speaking, people like to talk about themselves, and so it typically does not hurt to give the interviewer a chance to do just that. Jeff Fox, author of *How to Land Your Dream Job,* relates a story in which General Douglas MacArthur was looking to hire a new aide. A lieutenant interviewed for the position and pre-empted MacArthur by asking about his view of the army's role in the Pacific theater in World War II. Occasionally, the lieutenant interrupted to ask MacArthur to expand on what he was saying. MacArthur spoke for the vast majority of the interview and then offered the lieutenant the job, later telling a colonel that the lieutenant was one of the most intelligent people he had ever met. The lesson here is an important one. The lieutenant succeeded not so much by wowing MacArthur with personality and demonstrations of intelligence but by allowing MacArthur to enjoy the interview.

Much like the lieutenant in Fox's story, successful candidates often give the interview a more conversational tone by asking questions during the course of the interview rather than waiting until the end. In nearly every case it is better to ask questions during the course of the interview (as they naturally come to mind) than it is to wait until the end, when the interviewer will put you on the spot. When that happens, it is difficult to pose questions that seem natural.

CHAPTER 4

OVERVIEW OF THE
FINANCIAL WORLD

T o this point in the discussion, we primarily have discussed basic concepts that apply to nearly anyone seeking a job in nearly any field. We now shift the discussion to finance-specific topics that provide the basis for a candidate's substantive presentation during the interview. In this chapter, we focus on the role of investment banks and other financial institutions in society.

Finance is the science of allocating capital and putting it to use to generate more capital in the future. Financial institutions act as intermediaries in this process, collecting money from investors and providing it to companies and other organizations that need it. There are several broad categories of financial institutions, ranging from commercial banks, to insurance companies, to hedge funds. Although our primary focus is the **investment bank**, it is worth spending a few moments to describe a few other types of financial institutions.

COMMERCIAL BANKS

The most common form of financial institution is the **commercial bank**. A commercial bank collects deposits from individuals and organizations in exchange for a promised interest rate and gives out loans to individuals and organizations. A commercial bank makes most of its money by paying depositors a lower interest rate than it earns on its loans but also makes money by charging fees for other services (checking and ATMs, for example). *Savings and loans* and *thrifts* are very similar in their operations, although they are a bit different in focus and regulation.

> M&T Bank differs from many other organizations in that we look for both liberal arts students and business or finance students. Liberal arts students tend to be more creative, nimble, and open-minded, and we can always teach them the banking skills they need.
>
> —Robert Sadler, Jr.
> Former President and Chairman
> M&T Bank

RISK MANAGEMENT (INSURANCE) COMPANIES

Insurance companies are in many ways similar to commercial banks, although that is not obvious to most people. Like commercial banks, insurance companies collect money (called premiums) from individuals and organizations and invest those funds. Rather than promising investors an interest rate, however, insurance companies promise investors a **return** that depends on well-specified unfortunate events (e.g., auto accidents, restaurant fires). Insurance companies make money by paying their investors less in claims than those companies earn from premiums and investments.

ASSET MANAGERS

Mutual funds, hedge funds, and other asset managers collect investment funds from individuals and organizations in exchange for a future return that may or may not be specified in terms of amount or timing. Managers may invest those funds in a variety of assets, including stocks, bonds, real estate, and natural resources. In comparison to commercial banks and insurance companies, asset managers (particularly hedge funds) are relatively unregulated. Because of the lack of regulation, funds can make money in many different ways as long as investors agree to the compensation structure. For example, the manager of a hedge fund might be paid 2 percent of the fund amount each year plus 10 percent of the profits for the year.

INVESTMENT BANKS

Investment banks provide a variety of services to both organizations that need capital and investors looking to deploy capital. Entry-level jobs in investment banking typically last for two years and are at the *analyst* level. Analysts are responsible for basic financial analysis, preparation of pitch books, and almost anything else that might be needed. After two or three years, most analysts leave the bank to move on to another area of finance (such as **private equity**) or perhaps go to business school. A select few are offered the opportunity to continue with the bank and become *associates*. For the most part, associates have the same responsibilities as analysts, but associates do have the advantage of having analysts who work for them. In particular, associates participate in the analysis but also act as organizers and reviewers of the work of the analysts. After a few years of high-quality work, associates can be promoted to *vice president* and then to *managing director*. In one sense, vice presidents can be viewed as directors of the firm's financial analysis. They guide the activities of the analysts and associates and often are held responsible for any errors that are discovered in the analysis. Because vice presidents typically have in-depth knowledge of the analysis and have significant experience, they also spend a lot of time interacting with clients and potential clients. In contrast, managing directors generally do not have a detailed knowledge of the financial analysis done in a particular case but act as the face of the firm in terms of client interaction. They routinely interact with the highest-level employees at client firms and actively seek out new business for the bank.

It is difficult to categorize fully the types of services investment banks provide because companies sometimes need highly tailored solutions, but we can at least discuss some of the prominent areas. Readers should be aware that different investment banks often have different structures and use different terminology, and so what follows is a typical but not universal organizational structure.

Corporate Finance

The corporate finance division of a bank represents the core of investment banking. In fact, analysts in the corporate finance division are called *investment bankers* whereas analysts in other areas are called by other names, such as *traders* for analysts in sales and trading. Corporate finance typically is segmented into at least two and sometimes three areas: industry groups, product groups, and regional groups. It also often is segmented by its role, with employees in *mergers and acquisitions* (M&A) groups working with firms that wish to be sold or to buy other firms and *capital markets* groups working with firms that need to raise money by issuing debt or equity. When advising a company, *deal teams* are formed that consist of a lead high-level banker and representatives from industry, product, and perhaps regional groups. The size of the deal team and the number of representatives from each group depend on the deal in question. The corporate finance group makes money primarily by charging fees to clients.

Industry Groups. Analysts in an industry group work to understand a particular industry and the companies in it. They provide firm-specific and industry-specific expertise to the deal team. A bank's industry groups might consist of the following, although different banks may organize and assign titles differently:

- Health care
- Technology
- Telecommunications
- Natural resources
- Retail
- Financial institutions
- Financial sponsors (private equity groups)

Product Groups. Analysts in product groups work to develop expertise on a particular type of financing or deal structure. For example, they monitor the markets in their products so that they can determine the appropriate pricing for a proposed deal. A bank's product groups might be organized as follows:

- Debt
- Equity
- Mergers and acquisitions
- Leveraged finance (focus on highly leveraged deals, including leveraged buyouts [LBOs])
- Structured finance (focus on complex debt structures that divide and allocate risk)
- Syndicates (focus on large deals requiring multiple investment groups)

Wealth Management

Wealth managers in the bank provide advisory services to institutions (e.g., pension funds) and high-net-worth individuals. For example, a private wealth manager might work with a wealthy individual to develop an appropriate investment portfolio that satisfies that individual's needs and desires. Wealth managers make money not only by charging fees to clients but also by referring business to other areas of the bank.

Sales and Trading

Sales and trading groups are responsible for buying and selling securities on behalf of clients or on behalf of the bank itself. Most deals put together by corporate finance deal teams require the issuance of securities. For example, when a company hires an investment bank to prepare and execute an **initial public offering** (IPO), the bank creates shares to be sold to institutional investors (such as pension funds) and the general public. The sales and trading team then works to identify potential purchasers of the shares and get commitments from those potential investors to buy shares. Wealth managers also create business for the sales and trading team.

Like corporate finance, sales and trading is divided into different segments so that analysts can develop expertise in specific areas. For example, a *mortgage trading desk* is responsible for buying and selling securities that are based on pooled mortgages. The sales and trading team makes money by buying securities at one price and selling them at a higher price. Relationships are very important, however, and the bank may strategically choose to lose money on a deal in order to get the business of a particular company and develop a relationship with it. In doing so, the hope is that the company subsequently will use the bank for larger deals from which the bank will earn significant profits.

Research

The research division of an investment bank is responsible for analyzing companies and providing written assessments of the quality of the companies' outstanding securities (typically debt and equity). Research teams make money primarily by selling their research to asset managers and other outsiders but also by providing research to others in the bank who in turn generate profits. For example, wealth managers may use research reports from an equity analyst as a basis for developing an appropriate portfolio for a client.

Like corporate finance, the bank's research division often is split by industry and security type. For example, there may be a telecommunications group within the equity research portion of the research division.

PRIVATE EQUITY

Private equity firms engage in a variety of different strategies (e.g., venture capital, LBOs) in an effort to find and take advantage of potential value in privately held companies. Often, the private equity firm will take an active role in the management of the companies it buys in an effort to generate additional value through improved management practices. Although private equity firms generally do not hire students straight out of undergraduate school, they do regularly hire students straight out of MBA programs or hire former investment bankers and others who are looking to change their career path. In fact, many people go into investment banking with the explicit goal of using that banking experience as a launching pad to obtain a job in private equity.

OTHERS

There are other areas of finance, including brokerage, derivatives trading, and ratings analysis, among many others. The purpose of this book is not to discuss each area in detail but to present an overview of finance and discuss what it takes to get a job in financial services. Still, people interested in other areas will find that if they prepare as outlined here, they will be in good shape to interview for jobs in nearly all areas of finance.

CHAPTER 5

ACCOUNTING BASICS

Corporate financial analysis is largely dependent on forecasting the cash flows of companies, which in turn is dependent on the information reported by companies in their financial statements. Therefore, interviewers often ask questions designed to assess a candidate's understanding of the core financial statements: the balance sheet, the income statement, and the statement of cash flows. Although interviewers may ask a few questions to see whether candidates are familiar with the structure of those statements, they are more interested in discerning whether a candidate understands the linkages between the statements. Those linkages are important because an analyst must understand them to forecast financial statements that are internally consistent. With that in mind, it is worth discussing the statements briefly to understand their purpose and how they work together to paint a picture of a firm's operations.

THE BALANCE SHEET

The balance sheet (BS) shows the **book values** of a company's assets, liabilities, and equity at a particular point in time. The left-hand side lists the assets, and the right-hand side lists the company's liabilities and equity. Table 5.1 shows a sample BS. Brief descriptions of the accounts on that balance sheet follow. Readers should note that different companies use different accounting terminology, and so the accounts listed in Table 5.1 (and Tables 5.2 and 5.3) are not standard across companies.

Table 5.1: A Sample Balance Sheet

ASSETS	2008	2009
Cash	$120	$134
Receivable	$239	$251
Inventory	$412	$398
Other current assets	$67	$40
Total current assets	$838	$823
Goodwill	$200	$200
Accumulated amortization	$113	$124
Net Goodwill	$87	$76
PP&E	$580	$604
Accumulated depreciation	$116	$163
PP&E, Net	$464	$441
Other long-term assets	$23	$29
Total assets	$1,412	$1,369

LIABILITIES AND EQUITY	2008	2009
Accounts payable	$178	$213
Other current liabilities	$34	$21
Total current liabilities	$212	$234
Long-term debt	$317	$202
Total debt	$529	$436
Preferred stock	$0	$0
Common stock	$112	$118
Retained earnings	$771	$815
Total equity	$883	$933
Total liabilities & equity	$1,412	$1,369

See text for explanation of terms and acronyms.

Cash: The cash holdings of the company or holdings that can be converted immediately to cash without a loss of value.

Accounts receivable: A cumulative account that tracks sales that have been completed but for which the company has not yet been paid.

Inventory: An account that tracks the total amount of salable products the company currently has on hand. Inventory is recorded and maintained at its initial cost, and so no adjustments typically are made for any changes in the value of the inventory after it has been acquired.

Other current assets: A collection of miscellaneous current assets that do not naturally fit into the cash, receivables, or inventory account.

Goodwill: A cumulative account that tracks the difference between the amount paid for an acquired company and the book value of the acquired company. (After an acquisition, the acquiring company must include the target company's financial statements as part of the acquirer's financial statements, and so the goodwill adjustment is necessary to ensure that the balance sheet will still balance.) Goodwill can be written off (expensed) over time to potentially give the company a valuable tax break.

Accumulated amortization: An account (similar to accumulated depreciation) that tracks the total write-offs to date of goodwill.

Net goodwill: The net current book value of goodwill, which is calculated as goodwill less accumulated amortization.

PP&E: The value of a company's property, plant, and equipment recorded at their initial costs. With the exception of land, PP&E is gradually expensed on the income statement through the depreciation account.

Accumulated depreciation: An account that tracks the total depreciation write-offs to date.

PP&E, net: The net current book value of the company's PP&E, which is calculated as PP&E minus accumulated depreciation.

Other long-term assets: A collection of miscellaneous long-term assets that do not naturally fit into PP&E.

Accounts payable: A cumulative account that tracks the company's acquisitions of inventory that have been completed but for which the company has not yet paid.

Other current liabilities: A collection of miscellaneous long-term assets that do not naturally fit into payables.

Long-term debt: The current book value of the company's outstanding debt obligations. The account is not adjusted if the value of long-term debt changes after its issuance, and so its book value may deviate significantly from its market value.

Preferred stock: The current book value of the company's outstanding preferred stock obligations. The account is not adjusted if the value of preferred stock changes after its issuance, and so its book value may deviate significantly from its market value.

Common stock: The value of common stock, recorded at its par value (i.e., its initial stated value). The par value need not be what the stock initially was sold for, and so the book value of common stock may differ significantly from its market value.

Retained earnings: A cumulative account that tracks the accounting value of how much the common stock has changed in value as a result of accounting profits generated.

THE INCOME STATEMENT

The income statement (IS) shows the flow of operating values for the company. The term "operating values" is not a technical term but describes the purpose of the IS. A naive view of the IS is that it shows the operating cash flows of the firm, but it does not. Accounting rules dictate the circumstances in which events appear on the IS, and those rules in general do not require that there be cash receipts or disbursements for a transaction to be recorded on the IS. In contrast to the balance sheet, the IS covers a period of time (typically a quarter or a year) rather than a point in time. A sample IS is shown in Table 5.2. Brief descriptions of the accounts shown in Table 5.2 follow.

Table 5.2: A Sample Income Statement

	2009
Revenues	$2,810
COGS	$2,189
SG&A	$348
EBITDA	$273
D&A	$58
Operating income	$215
Other expenses	$17
EBIT	$198
Interest expense	$45
EBT	$153
Taxes	$49
Net income	$104
Dividends	$60
Additions to retained earnings	$44

See text for explanation of terms and acronyms.

Revenues: An account that records the value of goods or services sold during the year, recorded at the agreed-on purchase price. A sale is recorded when the good or service has been provided. This time is not necessarily the same time that payment is received for the good or service, and so revenues may not be equal to receipts from sales.

Cost of goods sold (COGS): An account that records the cost of any goods or services sold during the period. An entry to COGS is recorded whenever a sale is recorded. This is not necessarily the same time that the company pays for producing or acquiring the goods or services, and so COGS may not be equal to the actual payment made for the goods or services during the period.

SG&A: An account that records the company's expenses during the period for selling, general, and administrative activities.

Earnings before interest, taxes, depreciation, and amortization (EBITDA): An account that records the net operating flows for the company before deductions for depreciation, amortization, and other nonoperating expenses. EBITDA is a key measure on Wall Street because it approximates the actual value generated by the company during the period from the sale of goods and services.

D&A: An account that records write-offs for amortization (typically of goodwill) and depreciation of capital assets. Depreciation and amortization are non-cash flow expenses.

Other expenses: A collection of accounts that do not fit naturally into the previously mentioned accounts.

Earnings before interest and taxes (EBIT): A subtotal that captures the accounting value of profits generated during the period, before payments to debtholders and to the government (i.e., taxes).

Taxes: An account that records the company's obligation to the government for the period's activity.

Net income: An account that records the accounting value of profits generated by the company during the period.

Dividends: An account that records payments to shareholders during the period. Note that **dividends** normally do not appear on the income statement but instead appear on the statement of retained earnings. They are recorded here because for all intents and purposes they are a key part of the story told through the income statement.

Additions to retained earnings: An account that records the net value generated by the company for shareholders during the period. Additions to retained earnings are computed as net income minus dividends. Like dividends, additions to retained earnings do not normally appear on the income statement, but instead appear on the statement of retained earnings.

THE STATEMENT OF CASH FLOWS

Despite its name, the statement of cash flows (SCF) is not a list of a company's cash flows over a particular period. It is a document that converts a company's net income (the output of the income statement) into the actual cash flow of the company over the particular period. The entries on the SCF can be viewed as adjustments for items on the IS that are not cash flows or adjustments for cash flow items that do not appear on the IS at all. A sample SCF is shown in Table 5.3. Brief descriptions of the accounts shown in the table follow.

Table 5.3: A Sample Statement of Cash Flows

	2009
Net Income	$104
Cash flow (CF) from operating activities	
D&A	$58
Changes in A/R	–$12
Changes in inventory	$14
Changes in payables	$35
Other changes in operating activities	$14
CF from investing activities	
Capital expenditures	–$24
Investments	–$6
CF from financing activities	
Dividends	–$60
Sale/repurchase of stock	$6
Net borrowings	–$115
Changes in cash	$14

See text for explanation of terms and acronyms.

Net income: Carried over from the IS.

D&A: Carried over from the IS. Adjusts the net income for the fact that D&A was subtracted in the IS even though it is not cash flow.

Changes in accounts receivable: Inferred from the last two BSs. Adjusts the net income for the fact that revenues may include items for which the company has not yet been paid. Also adjusts the net income for any money the company received this period from sales that took place in prior periods.

Changes in inventory: Inferred from the last two BSs. Adjusts the net income for the fact that the company may have paid for new inventory during the period that the company has not sold yet. Also adjusts for the sale of inventory this period that was acquired during a prior period.

Changes in payables: Inferred from the last two BSs. Adjusts the net income for the fact that the firm may have sold inventory that it has not paid for yet. Also adjusts the net income for any money the company has spent to pay off payables that were incurred in prior periods.

Other changes in operating activities: Inferred from the last two BSs. Captures miscellaneous effects similar to the receivables, inventory, and payables effects.

Capital expenditures: Adjusts the net income for money spent to acquire capital assets (which ordinarily does not show up on the IS).

Investments: Adjusts the net income for money spent to acquire investment assets (e.g., stock in other companies), which ordinarily does not show up on the IS.

Dividends: Adjusts the net income for money paid to shareholders as compensation for the use of their funds.

Sale/repurchase of stock: Adjusts the net income for money received from the issuance of new stock or money used to buy back existing stock, both of which ordinarily do not appear on the IS.

Net borrowings: Adjusts the net income for money received from the issuance of new debt or money used to buy back existing debt, both of which ordinarily do not appear on the IS.

Because the SCF tends to receive less attention than the BS and IS, interviewers often question candidates about their knowledge of the SCF.

SIQ26: *What is the first line of the statement of cash flows? What is the last line?*

Questions like SIQ26 are of course easy, but they are missed far more often than one might expect. In particular, candidates often reply that the first line of the SCF is revenues. An incorrect answer to questions like these all but assures that the candidate will not get the job. After all, the bank is looking for candidates who have at least taken the time to learn a bit about the fundamentals of the job.

LINKAGES BETWEEN THE FINANCIAL STATEMENTS

Financial forecasting involves creating pro forma financial statements, or predictions of the company's financial statements for the years to come. To forecast financials, an analyst must understand the relationships between the statements. As a result, interviewers often explore these relationships with the candidate. Questions such as the following are common:

> SIQ27: *How does depreciation affect the main financial statements?*
> SIQ28: *How are the main financial statements connected?*

It is beyond the scope of this book to go through each and every connection between the financial statements. Still, it is worthwhile to make two key observations about those connections:

✦ The statement of cash flows can be viewed as the change in the balance sheet. In fact, each and every item on the SCF depicts a change in the BS. This is obvious for some accounts, such as the change in receivables, but not so obvious for others. For example, net income appears on the SCF but does not seem to appear on the BS. Similarly, dividends appear on the SCF but not on the BS. Notice, however, that the difference between net income and dividends is the company's retained earnings, which is accumulated on the BS as part of common equity. Thus, the difference between net income and dividends is a change in common equity on the BS.

✦ A change in any account typically will affect many other accounts on all three statements. For example, how would a $100 increase in depreciation affect the financial statements? A good but incomplete answer is to say that it appears directly on the IS and the SCF and is accumulated on the BS as a reduction of property, plant, and equipment. This communicates to the interviewer that the candidate is familiar with the basic connections, but it also wastes an opportunity for the candidate to shine. To see this, the following is a list of all the changes to the three statements when depreciation increases by $100, assuming that the company's tax rate is 30 percent.

Changes to the Income Statement

- ✦ Depreciation increases by $100.
- ✦ Taxable income decreases by $100.
- ✦ Taxes decrease by $30 (30 percent of $100).
- ✦ Net income decreases by $70.

Changes to the Balance Sheet

- ✦ Cash increases by $30 (since the company pays $30 less in taxes).
- ✦ Accumulated depreciation increases by $100.
- ✦ Property, plant, and equipment decreases by $100.
- ✦ Total assets decreases by $70.
- ✦ Retained earnings decreases by $70.
- ✦ Total liabilities and equity decreases by $70.

Changes to the Statement of Cash Flows

- ✦ Net income decreases by $70.
- ✦ Depreciation increases by $100.
- ✦ Changes in cash increases by $30.

Perhaps the most important point of this example is that it illustrates the intricate connectivity of the financial statements. A small change in one account can have widespread implications for all the financial statements. Successful candidates are the ones who understand this and can articulate it quickly and efficiently.

CHAPTER 6

FINANCE BASICS

Interviewers typically spend time exploring the depth of a candidate's knowledge of finance. The standard by which the candidate is judged depends on the candidate's background, and so there are no rules specifying what the candidate must know to get the job. There are many people working today on Wall Street who got their jobs with very little knowledge of finance. Still, the more a candidate knows about finance, the greater the likelihood of a job offer is.

Successful financial analysts have a solid understanding of four basic concepts in finance: (1) the time value of money, (2) the risk-return relationship, (3) capital structure, and (4) valuation. We will discuss the first three of these concepts in this chapter, but only in broad terms; valuation is treated in detail in Chapter 7. Readers interested in developing a more in-depth understanding should consult other resources, some of which are described later in this book, and take relevant coursework when possible.

THE TIME VALUE OF MONEY

Employers expect candidates to have at least a rudimentary understanding of the time value of money. With that in mind, it is useful for candidates to know three simple equations and how to apply them:

(6.1) *Value of a single cash flow expected in t periods =*
$$C_t/(1 + R)^t$$
(6.2) *Value of a perpetuity = C/R*
(6.3) *Value of a* **perpetual growth** *security = C/(R − g)*

A **perpetuity** is a security that pays a specified amount each period forever, whereas a growing perpetuity is a perpetuity with cash flows that grow at a fixed rate (*g* in this case) each period. In all three equations, *R* is the appropriate per-period interest rate expressed as a decimal instead of a percentage (0.08 instead of 8 percent, for example). In Equation 6.1, C_t is the cash flow to be received in *t* periods. In Equation 6.2, *C* is the amount of the repeating cash flow: $100 per year, for example. In Equation 6.3, *C* is the first cash flow of the security, with each subsequent cash flow being larger by the rate *g* than the one before it. It is important to recognize that both equations 6.2 and 6.3 are based on the assumption that the first cash flow is expected one period from today.

The next section will discuss the meaning and application of the interest rate *R* and describe briefly how it is determined. For now, readers should assume that *R* is given. There are numerous resources, including many online, that provide sample problems requiring the use of the three equations. Here we will just highlight a few that are asked frequently in interviews. Each subsequent question is slightly more difficult than the one before it and all questions are designed to test the candidate's basic knowledge of the time value of money. Interviewers interested in digging deeper into a candidate's knowledge sometimes follow the simple questions with more complicated ones to see how deep that knowledge is.

SIQ29: *Suppose I offer to pay you $100 in one year.*
If the interest rate is 8 percent annually, what is my offer
worth to you today? What if the cash flow is instead to
be paid in three years?

SIQ30: *Suppose a security pays $1 every year forever, with the first dollar to be paid in one year. If the interest rate is 10 percent annually, what is the security worth today? What if the first cash flow is to be paid today instead of in one year?*

SIQ31: *Suppose a company plans to pay a stock dividend of $1 next year and you expect the dividend to increase by 3 percent each year thereafter. If the interest rate is 7 percent annually, what is the stock worth to you today?*

Readers should verify that the answers to these questions are SIQ29: $92.59, $79.38; SIQ30: $10, $11 ($1 more than in the first part because the extra dollar paid today is worth precisely $1 today); and SIQ31: $25. In interviews, of course, candidates would not be expected to compute these values to the penny but would be expected to explain how to do the calculation and then give a rough approximation of the answer.

There are no special tricks to these problems, and it is not a significant plus if the candidate can answer them. Instead, the questions provide opportunities for the candidate to lose points by answering incorrectly or by not being able to answer at all. Perhaps the best approach to answering is to begin by stating the equation briefly and then offer the amount. That way, even if the candidate happens to miscalculate the answer, the interviewer will know that the candidate knows what he or she is doing. For example, the candidate might provide the following answer to SIQ31: "Well, the value of a growing perpetuity is the cash flow divided by the difference between the interest rate and the growth rate. In this case, the value would be $1 divided by 0.04, or $25." Answers like these are more expressive and show both knowledge and thought process. Again, successful candidates tend to take advantage of each and every opportunity to show what they know.

THE RISK-RETURN RELATIONSHIP

In the previous section, we discussed some simple time value of money relationships and how interviewers might present them to candidates. The equations describing those relationships require a discount rate. In theory, the **discount rate** for a particular security is nothing more than the interest rate an investor can expect to receive on alternative securities of equivalent risk. For example, suppose that a security pays $110 in one year and that other securities with similar risk are expected to **return** 10 percent per year. We say that the value of the $110 security is $110/1.1 = $100. The math is of course easy. More important is to understand the intuition; no one would pay more than $100 for the security because that would reduce the return to below 10 percent. If the security were selling for more than $100, a wise investor would choose one of the alternative investments instead. This would reduce the demand for the security, which in theory would result in a decrease in its price. In equilibrium, the price would drop to $100, at which time the supply and demand in the marketplace would be equal.

A key element in this discussion is the notion of equivalent risk. A fundamental premise of finance is that if one security is riskier than another, investors must expect a higher reward from the riskier security or they will not buy it. Measuring the risk of an asset is somewhat more difficult, but there are two commonly used measures:

✦ Standard deviation of returns = statistical measure of the *total risk* of an asset

✦ **Beta** = statistical measure of the *relevant risk* of an asset

Beta is the theoretically relevant measure for individual assets, whereas both beta and the standard deviation are reasonable measures for well-diversified portfolios.

THE CAPITAL ASSET PRICING MODEL (CAPM)

Some risk is not relevant in asset pricing because it can be avoided by holding a diversified portfolio. Such risk is called **diversifiable risk**. Beta measures the risk that remains after all diversifiable risk is removed. This risk is called *market risk* or **nondiversifiable risk**. The importance of beta is that it allows us to express a relationship between the expected return on an asset and the asset's relevant risk. The relationship is called the *capital asset pricing model* (*CAPM*) and is expressed as follows:

$$(6.4)\ E(R) = R_f + B \times (E(R_m) - R_f)$$

In words, the CAPM says the expected return on an asset is equal to the **risk-free rate** of return plus a risk premium that is the product of beta and the **market risk premium**. The market risk premium is the difference between the expected return on the market portfolio and the risk-free rate. In theory, the market portfolio is a portfolio of all assets weighted according to their **market values**. The CAPM is important because it allows us (in theory) to compute the minimum return that investors would need to be compensated for the relevant risk associated with the security. Thus, this expected return is the appropriate interest rate for time value of money calculations. The CAPM is useful in situations in which the interest rate on a security is not readily observable. In finance, the equation most often is used for common stock and seldom is used for other securities, such as bonds and preferred stock.

Interviewers may ask candidates to explain the CAPM or even write it down. They also have been known to ask the candidate to do a simple problem such as the following:

SIQ32: *Suppose the risk-free rate is 4 percent and the market risk premium is 5 percent. If a security has a beta of 1.2, what is the appropriate discount rate to use in valuing the security?*

Readers should verify that the correct answer is 10 percent. As in several previous sample questions, there is little for the candidate to gain but much to lose. Also, candidates should listen carefully to numerical questions about the CAPM because the interviewer might provide the expected market return instead of the market risk premium. In SIQ32, for example, the interviewer might say that the expected market return is 9 percent in lieu of giving the 5 percent market risk premium. More difficult questions about the CAPM concern how to estimate some of the key components.

SIQ33: *How would you go about estimating the risk-free rate? What about the market risk premium?*

Betas are estimated by data service companies and are readily available online. The risk-free rate is the interest rate investors would receive on a security with no risk. The closest things we have to a risk-free security are U.S. Treasury securities, and so we would use the interest rate on one of them (typically a 5- or 10-year bond) as an estimate of the risk-free rate. The market risk premium is more difficult to estimate, but banks typically use something on the order of 5 percent for their calculations.

Now that we know a bit about the risk-return relationship, it is worth recasting SIQ30 as it often is asked by interviewers.

SIQ34: *Suppose I offer to pay you $1 every year forever. What is it worth to you today?*

At first glance, this question is much like the earlier questions. Like the others, surely there is little for the candidate to gain and much to lose. There are a few subtle differences between this question and the others, however, and the candidate has an opportunity to turn the interview very much to his or her advantage. First, note that the interviewer has not specified when the payments begin. Second, note that the interviewer has not specified a discount rate. With this in mind, how should a candidate approach this question and others like it? Most candidates focus on getting to the right answer quickly. They ask for an interest rate (suppose the response is 10 percent) and then provide an answer ($10 in this case) with no explanation. There is nothing wrong with this, but candidates taking this approach pass up a valuable opportunity. Note first that a candidate who just answers "$10" implicitly assumes that the first payment will be in one year. A better approach is to state the assumption explicitly by saying something like "$10 if the first payment is to be paid in one year." This subtly lets the interviewer know that the candidate pays attention to details, which is a key characteristic of a good banker. Perhaps more important, the interviewer has given the candidate an opportunity to demonstrate an understanding of risk and return. Instead of asking for a discount rate, the candidate could take command of the interview by saying, "I would need to evaluate how risky you are in order to determine an appropriate discount rate. Let's suppose I do so and come up with 10 percent. Then the security would be worth $10 assuming that the first cash flow is to be paid in one year." This is a powerful way to gain points in the interview. The interviewer is not going to respond by sitting back and saying "Wow!" or immediately offering the candidate a job, but rest assured that the interviewer will take away a positive impression of the candidate's attention to detail and understanding of the time value of money.

The point of this discussion is not to encourage candidates to memorize "good" answers to the common questions but to encourage them to think carefully about their answers and be precise in what they say. That allows the interviewer to observe the candidate's thought process, which is the main objective of the interview.

THE WEIGHTED AVERAGE COST OF CAPITAL (WACC)

To finance its operations, the company collects money from debtholders, preferred stockholders, and common stockholders in exchange for a promise of future returns. To value the company, we need somehow to take into account the returns those investors expect to receive from the company. In the previous section, we discussed the importance of the CAPM in determining the discount rate on common stock. In valuing the entire company, however, we also must consider the company's other forms of financing: debt and preferred stock. Fortunately, the interest rate on debt typically is easy to estimate. Current market prices for the company's debt and the promised cash flows on the company's debt allow us to compute the implied interest rate on the debt. This rate is called the **yield to maturity** (or simply the yield). The yield reflects the interest rate investors would receive if they bought the debt today, held it to maturity, and received all the promised cash flows as scheduled. The interest rate on preferred stock is also relatively easy to estimate since preferred stock is a perpetuity. The current market price for the preferred stock and the promised preferred stock dividend allow us to infer the interest rate by using Equation 6.2. For example, if a company's preferred stock pays a $2 annual dividend and sells for $25, the interest rate is $2/$25 = 8 percent.

The **weighted average cost of capital** (WACC) is simply the weighted average interest rate on the company's outstanding debt, preferred stock, and common stock. The WACC equation is straightforward:

$$(6.5) \quad WACC = w_D R_D (1 - T) + w_{PS} R_{PS} + w_{CS} R_C,$$

Where w_D, w_{PS}, and w_{CS} are the weights on debt, preferred stock, and common stock; R_D, R_{PS}, and R_{CS} are the interest rates (i.e., required returns) on debt, preferred stock, and common stock; and T is the company's marginal tax rate. In the equation, the term representing debt is multiplied by $1 - T$ to adjust for the fact that interest payments on debt are tax-deductible. The weights in the equation are the respective fractions of the company's total financing contributed by debt, preferred stock, and common stock. For example, if the company has $100 of debt, $50 of preferred stock, and $250 of common stock ($400 of total financing), the weights on debt, preferred stock, and common stock would be 25 percent, 12.5 percent, and 62.5 percent, respectively. These weights are computed by using the market values of debt, preferred stock, and common stock whenever possible.

The WACC is a common topic in interviews, particularly for seniors seeking jobs. Juniors generally are expected to know what the WACC is but would not be expected to know it inside and out. Seniors, in contrast, are expected to be able to dissect the formula carefully. Of course, the extent of this expectation depends on the candidate's background in finance. Common interview questions include the following:

SIQ35: *What discount rate would you use in the DCF model?*

SIQ36: *What is the WACC? Can you write it down for me?*

We will discuss the DCF model in Chapter 7. Suffice to say that the WACC is the appropriate discount for that model. Common mistakes include forgetting the tax effect on debt. Such mistakes are major ones because the interviewer is left to wonder whether the candidate forgot to include the tax effect or does not know that the interest tax deduction is one of the fundamental advantages of debt.

CAPITAL STRUCTURE

Capital structure is by definition the makeup of the company's financing. In simple terms, we can view it as the weights that were identified in the WACC equation. Capital structure is a bit more complicated than that, however, because there are many different kinds of debt. It is well beyond the scope of this book to discuss the myriad choices available to the firm, but it is worthwhile to discuss the basic features of debt, preferred stock, and common stock briefly.

Debt

Debt is characterized by cash obligations that are prespecified in amount and timing. Debt can be quite complicated, though, in that many different structures and provisions may be employed. For example, bonds may be callable (giving the company the right to buy back a bond at a prespecified price) or convertible (giving the buyer of a bond the right to exchange the bond for a prespecified number of shares of stock). For the purposes of this discussion, however, we focus on a few key characteristics of debt:

1. Debt is senior to preferred stock and common stock, and so debtholders must be paid before stockholders can be paid dividends.
2. Interest payments on debt are tax-deductible.
3. Debtholders sometimes have the right to seize company assets if the company defaults on the debt.

The implication of the first characteristic is that debt is generally safer than equity (stock). Therefore, the interest rate on debt typically is lower than the returns expected by stockholders. The implication of the second characteristic is that the government provides a subsidy (in the form of lower taxes) to companies that choose to finance with debt. The first two characteristics taken together suggest that debt can be a very cheap form of financing. The third characteristic is the drawback, implying that debtholders potentially can force the company into bankruptcy. Understanding these characteristics is important to candidates facing questions such as SIQ19 (*Which is cheaper, debt or equity?*).

Preferred Stock

Preferred stock is somewhat of a misnomer because it is in most respects more like debt than it is like equity. A few key characteristics of preferred stock are as follows:

1. Preferred stock is senior to common stock but junior to debt, and so debtholders must be paid before preferred stockholders and preferred stockholders typically must be paid before common stockholders.
2. Preferred stock dividends are generally not tax deductible.
3. Preferred stockholders typically do not have voting rights.
4. Preferred stockholders typically do not have the right to seize company assets if a company misses dividend payments.

Generally speaking, one key advantage of preferred stock is that preferred stockholders cannot force the company into bankruptcy. The cost of this advantage is that the company in most situations gives up the interest tax deduction when it chooses preferred stock over debt.

Common Stock

Common stock is the residual claim on the company, meaning that common stockholders get paid last. Key characteristics of common stock are as follows:

1. Common stock is junior to all other financing claims.

2. Common stock dividends are generally not tax-deductible.

3. Common stockholders have voting rights that allow them to elect the company's board of directors. The board in turn hires company management (CEO, etc.), and so voting rights can be very important.

A primary advantage of common stock over debt and preferred stock is that the company is under no legal obligation ever to pay a dividend on common stock. This gives the company a great deal of flexibility, but there are several disadvantages associated with common stock. First, if the company issues additional shares of common stock to raise needed funds, the shares that belong to original shareholders are *diluted* (meaning that the original shares constitute a smaller percentage of the company). This can be quite problematic if control of the company is at stake. By issuing debt or preferred stock, the company can avoid this dilution effect. Second, companies financing with common stock are not able to take advantage of the interest tax deduction of debt. Third, company managers who issue additional common stock subsequently have a greater pool of shareholders to please. Fourth, issuing additional common stock sends a signal to the market that the common stock may be overvalued. After all, would the company opt to sell shares of stock if the stock was trading at some price below its true value?

There are many other pros and cons we might discuss. Our purpose, however, is not to be exhaustive but to provide candidates with some basic information that might prove useful in interviews. Readers interested in learning more about the capital structure choice can consult any of a number of online and paper resources dealing with the topic.

CHAPTER 7

VALUING COMPANIES

A common theme in many finance-related jobs is the valuation of companies. Financial analysts value companies, value the securities of companies, or use valuations put together by other financial analysts. Because of this, valuation is a common theme in interviews. For the most part, candidates are not expected to be able to produce complex models to estimate a company's value. They are, however, expected to know the basic approaches and the intuition behind them. There are three approaches candidates should be familiar with. Different banks often use different terminology to describe these approaches, but *trading comps, transaction comps,* and *DCF* are fairly common labels. In addition, candidates can demonstrate knowledge beyond the usual by showing an understanding of *LBO analysis.*

SIQ37: *How would you go about valuing a stock?*

For juniors, it is probably sufficient to be able to name the approaches and briefly describe them. For seniors, candidates professing to know something about the approaches can expect detailed questions about each technique, in particular the DCF model. When looking to hire people with finance experience, some firms even ask candidates to build a DCF model for a specific firm. Because valuation is so important to the financial services industry and therefore to the interviewing process, we will discuss each model in this chapter.

TRADING COMPS

A simple way to value entire companies or the stocks of companies is to rely on **market multiples**. The basic intuition is that similar companies should have similar market multiples. For example, suppose that a company has earnings of $3 per share and that the stocks of peer companies trade at a median of 14 times their levels of earnings (i.e., the median P/E ratio is 14). We can reasonably estimate the value of the company's stock to be $42 (i.e., $3 × 14). There are no tricks here—the technique really is as simple as it appears. Still, there are a few things to consider. First, the choice of similar companies is an important one. A good comp is one that is in the same industry as the company being valued, with similar size, debt ratio, geography, and so on. The catch, of course, is that companies want to differentiate themselves from one another. It follows that good comps can be difficult (and sometimes impossible) to find. Second, the choice of a market multiple is important. We generally rely on several different multiples and use them collectively to get a sense of the value of a company. Still, there are good multiples and bad ones. Good multiples are generally ones with a measure of value in the numerator and a measure of some factor that contributes to that value in the denominator. The price-to-earnings ratio and the ratio of **enterprise value** (EV) to **earnings before interest, taxes, depreciation, and amortization (EBITDA)** are used commonly in part because their numerators are consistent with their denominators. Earnings are a measure of the profits generated for shareholders, and the share price is the market value of a share. Thus, both the numerator and the denominator of the price/earnings (P/E) ratio deal with the company's equity. EBITDA is a measure of the profits generated to be distributed to both debtholders and equityholders, whereas enterprise value measures the value of the entire company. Thus, both the numerator and the denominator of the EV/EBITDA ratio deal with the entire company (not just the equity).

Trading comps are useful in trying to determine what price a stock (or an entire company) is likely to have in the open market. For example, an investment bank that is advising a company on a potential initial public offering (IPO) often will use trading comps to estimate what price the stock will trade for when it is public. The trading comps concept is also a component of the DCF model, which we will discuss later in this chapter.

TRANSACTION COMPS

Analyzing a potential mergers and acquisition (M&A) transaction is a bit more difficult than estimating a potential market price for a stock. This is the case because the acquiring company will have to pay a premium above the target's current stock price to acquire enough shares to take control of the target. Basic economics teaches that this high demand for the target's stock will push its price up, leading to the purchase premium. It follows that analysts cannot reasonably use trading comps to estimate the purchase price of a proposed acquisition. Instead, a close variation is used.

Transaction comps are identical to trading comps except that instead of using current market values in the numerator of the multiples, purchase prices from historical M&A transactions are used. Ideally, these transactions are ones that took place in the target company's industry, but analysts sometimes look elsewhere if there is a specific need to do so. By using historical mergers and acquisitions, the analyst can, at least in theory, obtain reasonable estimates for a new proposed transaction. The major drawback of transaction comps is that there may be few or no recent historical transactions in the industry. In these situations, analysts must rely on more complicated approaches to estimate company value.

THE DISCOUNTED CASH FLOW (DCF) MODEL

The DCF model is an attempt to measure the value of the company directly instead of relying on comparison to a peer group. The model incorporates much of the intuition we have already covered, most notably in that we use market multiples, the WACC, and the idea of converting net income into a measure of cash flow. The simple statement of the DCF is that it involves forecasting the **free cash flows** of the firm and then discounting them by using the WACC. In practice, this is much more difficult than it sounds.

Free Cash Flows. Our desire in the DCF model is to forecast the cash flows of the company, but what cash flows should we forecast? Recall that the WACC is a measure of the return the company must generate to satisfy its investors. The DCF model involves discounting cash flows by using the WACC, and so the discounting process specifically takes into account the return to investors. Therefore, the cash flows we forecast must *not* include payments to investors. If those payments were included, we would effectively be double counting the return to investors. The implication of this is that we must forecast all the cash flows of the company except for any cash flows related to the financing of the company (e.g., dividends, interest payments). These cash flows are called *free cash flows* (*FCF*) and can be estimated by using the following equation:

$$(7.1)\ FCF = \textbf{EBIT}(1-T) + D\&A - changes\ in\ NWC - CapEx + other\ effects$$

The first term, EBIT$(1-T)$, is the net income the company would have if it had no debt. We begin with this instead of net income because free cash flow is by construction independent of the company's financing. We therefore must remove the impact of any interest expense. Depreciation and amortization are added to offset their subtraction on the income statement (recall that

D&A are noncash expenses). Net working capital (NWC) is the company's current assets minus its current liabilities, and so it includes accounts such as receivables, inventory, and payables. We subtract changes in NWC to adjust for three main effects. First, an increase in accounts receivable implies that the company has recorded sales for which it has not received payment. In that case, revenues on the income statement would include sales for which the company has not yet received payment. We subtract the increase in accounts receivable to offset these sorts of sales. Second, the company's cost of goods sold (COGS) might include inventory items that the company has acquired but has not paid for yet. In that case, COGS on the income statement would overestimate the actual amount paid for sold goods during the period. We subtract the decrease in accounts payable (i.e., add any increase in payables) to offset this effect. Third, the company may have bought inventory during the period that has not been sold yet. The cost of the inventory would be a cash expense for the company, but it does not show up on that period's income statement because the new inventory has not been sold yet. We adjust for this by subtracting the increase in inventory. The adjustments for accounts receivable, accounts payable, and inventory typically are captured all at once by forecasting the changes in net working capital. Finally, we subtract the company's capital expenditures because they reflect cash payments of the company that do not appear on that period's income statement. There may be other effects as well, such as expenses related to goodwill.

The DCF model is perhaps the most theoretically attractive valuation approach we have, but applying it in the real world is a bit problematic. The biggest difficulty is that the company in theory could generate cash flows forever. We therefore would need to forecast the company's free cash flows forever to obtain an accurate estimate of value. This is clearly impossible. To avoid this, the DCF procedure calls for the forecasting of a finite number of free cash flows (typically 10 or so) along with a terminal value (TV) that captures the value of free cash flows the company might generate after the end of the forecast period. Table 7.1 depicts this structure for a forecast period of N years.

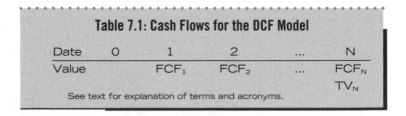

Date	0	1	2	...	N
Value		FCF_1	FCF_2	...	FCF_N
					TV_N

See text for explanation of terms and acronyms.

The Terminal Value. In theory, the terminal value, which is expressed as (TV_N) in Table 7.1, is the present value of the company's free cash flows from year $N + 1$ on. In practice, of course, we must find a different way to estimate that terminal value. There are two commonly used approaches, both of which we already have examined. The first is to use the perpetual growth formula (Equation 6.3). The second is to apply the trading comps intuition.

The perpetual growth equation requires a long-term growth rate, but estimating such a growth rate accurately is at best a very difficult task. We do know that it pays to be conservative in choosing the rate because the perpetual growth equation assumes an infinite number of cash flows, which is impossible. Estimates in the range of 0 to 2 percent are reasonable and are used commonly by analysts. In most situations, the choice is largely arbitrary. This is unfortunate because the choice can have a significant impact on the value estimate.

The trading comps approach typically is implemented by using the market multiple EV/FCF or perhaps EV/EBITDA. It proceeds just as we described earlier, but with the added complication of having to estimate what the industry EV/FCF is likely to be in N years. For a company in a stable industry, we can simply use a recent historical average or something of that nature. For a company in an industry in flux, a "best guess" estimate is typical.

Putting It All Together. Once we have forecast the free cash flows and the terminal value, we need only discount them by using the WACC to obtain an estimate of the value of the company. If we are interested in the value of the company's common stock, we would subtract the values of **net debt** and preferred stock from our estimate of company value to get the estimate of stock value.

The DCF model has the disadvantage that the terminal value typically contributes a large portion of the overall value of the company. Thus, the accuracy of the DCF model depends heavily on the accuracy of the estimate of the terminal value. Both the perpetual growth approach and the market multiple approach lead to estimates that tend to be highly uncertain. As a result, the DCF model does not allow us to make a reasonable estimate of the value of the company's stock. Rather, it allows us to estimate a range of values for the company's stock. We do this by considering multiple possibilities for the key assumptions so that we can get a feel for how high or low the true value might be.

LBO Analysis

A *leveraged buyout* occurs when a group of investors purchase a controlling interest in a company while using a large amount of debt to finance the transaction. The debt is paid off over the next few years by using the company's free cash flows. Once the debt is paid off, the investors own a significantly higher portion of the company, resulting in very high returns if things go as planned. An example illustrates the process. For simplicity, we will consider an all-equity firm in the example, but the target firm need not be financed entirely with equity. Furthermore, for simplicity we will assume that the entire company is purchased. In reality, investors would only need to buy a controlling interest in the company to execute an LBO strategy.

Suppose that a company can be purchased for $100 million. The company currently generates high and stable free cash flows, and so debtholders are willing to lend $80 million toward the purchase of the company while equity investors provide the remaining $20 million. An interesting feature of most LBOs is that the debt used to purchase the company is repaid by the company itself. The debt is issued simultaneously with the purchase, and the company, rather than the equity investors, is on the hook to repay it. The debt is paid down gradually over the coming years, giving equityholders a larger and larger ownership claim over time. Suppose, for example, that the debt is amortized at 7 percent annual interest over 10 years. The annual debt payment would be roughly $11.4 million. Consider the situation five years after the LBO. The company would still owe roughly $46.7 million on the debt. Suppose then that the company is still worth $100 million at that time. That is, suppose that the company's growth was stagnant in the five years that followed the LBO. Equityholders, who invested $20 million, would hold shares worth roughly $53.3 million even though the company had not grown in value at all. That amounts to about a 22 percent annual return over the period. This is the beauty of the LBO. Using the company's free cash flows to pay down the debt can generate significant returns to equityholders. Even better, suppose that the company grows in value to, say, $140 million over the five years (an annual growth rate of about 7 percent). Equityholders will hold shares worth $93.3 million, which represents a staggering annual return of 36 percent. With potential returns that high, it is easy to see why LBOs are a popular investment vehicle.

Although undergraduate candidates generally are not expected to know anything about LBOs, they are well advised to understand the basics of the LBO model. Since few undergraduates have exposure to LBOs, demonstrating an understanding of them can greatly increase the probability of getting the job offer. For example, several years ago one of my students sought my advice about interviewing for a job in investment banking on Wall Street. As a history major, he had only a casual understanding of the DCF model and in fact felt uncomfortable when trying to explain it. We worked through the LBO model together and then talked about a few companies that appeared to be good LBO targets because of their high and stable free cash flows. When the student subsequently interviewed with a major New York bank, he was asked how to go about valuing a company.

He wisely mentioned comps and the DCF model but shifted the conversation to LBOs in an effort to talk about what he understood best. The interviewer then asked what companies the student had been looking at. He again wisely shifted the focus to LBOs by mentioning a specific company and explaining why it would be a good LBO candidate. He received a full-time job offer from the bank that day.

In contrast, candidates who have been out of school a few years probably will be expected to know the LBO model quite well. In all areas, the bar is set higher for more senior candidates simply because the competition includes many who already have extensive experience. One way to display a solid understanding of the model quickly is to point out that purchasing a house with a large mortgage is roughly equivalent to an LBO. The debt retirement over time generates returns to the homeowner even if the house price does not increase much.

CHAPTER 8

RECENT FINANCIAL EVENTS

In Chapters 5, 6, and 7, we considered how one might use accounting information to estimate the value of a stock. Successful job candidates typically have at least some knowledge of the information in those chapters, but they also usually have general knowledge of the economic factors that influence events on Wall Street. The purpose of this chapter is to provide candidates with a high-level perspective on recent financial events, with special emphasis on the recent real estate crisis. In doing this, our hope is that the candidate will build a base to draw on in interviews. The discussion is not meant to be a comprehensive or exhaustive treatment of the subject. Such a treatment would require far more space than is available here. Furthermore, candidates need not be experts on any particular facet of the following discussion. Rather, they should have a basic sense of how various factors work together to trigger significant economic events. As we discussed earlier, such an understanding may prove useful both during the interview process (as the candidate interacts with employers) and afterward (as the newly hired employee interacts with potential clients).

Although the focus will be on the subprime mortgage crisis and related events of the 2000s, it is useful to start by talking about the **dot-com bubble** that preceded it. Although it is difficult to date the start of any bubble, one event typifies the volatility and uncertainty that led to the dot-com bubble. The Internet existed for decades before its public emergence in the 1990s. By the early 1990s, technology had advanced to the point where a public network became both viable and desirable. In the early days of the Internet, the browser segment of the industry was dominated by the browsers Mosaic and Netscape, with Netscape seemingly having the edge in user preference. On August 9, 1995, Netscape initiated an IPO, offering its stock to the public for the first time. Reports suggested that the stock was to be offered at $14 per share, but that was doubled at the last minute because of the perception that demand for the stock would be high. The stock climbed as high as about $75 that first day before settling back a bit to close at $58.25. Over the next few months, the stock climbed to a peak in excess of $170 and then fell back to a "normal" level of just over $40 per share (Figure 8.1).

The Netscape story is important because the stock's market value was based almost entirely on speculation. The company had no real revenues and no real prospects for revenues, yet investors purchased the stock in droves with the expectation that the company one day would figure out a way to turn the magic of the Internet into dollars or that someone else (a "greater fool") would come along behind them to purchase the stock at an even higher price. In other words, Netscape stock was a bubble that foreshadowed the dot-com bubble that arose over the next few years. During that bubble, companies with any sort of connection to the Internet found great favor in the marketplace. Those

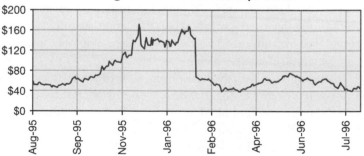

Figure 8.1: Price of Netscape Stock

Data from Center for Research in Security Pricing

companies raised great sums of money with no apparent means to repay investors. The returns were dramatic over the first few years of the bubble, leading to a strange sort of equilibrium in the mutual fund world. Although a significant number of mutual fund managers recognized the bubble, the general public did not. That situation forced many fund managers to continue buying tech stocks or risk having investors withdraw their money to invest it in tech-heavy funds. This effect tended to prolong the bubble rather than mitigate its effects.

It is easy to look back on the Netscape bubble and think that we, the enlightened twenty-first-century investment community, would have not been taken in by the folly of Netscape. After all, we understand what a bubble is and surely would be able to identify one as it happened. Burton Malkiel addressed this idea in his iconic book *A Random Walk down Wall Street,* in which he, among other things, documented the long history of bubbles around the world. For example, Malkiel related the story of the tulip bulb craze in Holland. The short version of the story is that the citizens of Holland became so enamored with tulips that a bubble lasting decades formed, with people eventually trading their land and other possessions for the most beautiful tulip bulbs. Prices increased twentyfold in January 1637 alone, leading to the collapse of the bubble shortly thereafter. As Malkiel seems to suggest, there are a few near certainties concerning bubbles. First, bubbles inevitably collapse and do so without warning. Although some people no doubt get lucky and make money as the bubble expands, others get caught as the bubble pops and prices plummet. Second, to date we do not seem to have learned the lessons from the long history of documented bubbles. Until we do, bubbles are likely to recur from time to time, often leaving economies in turmoil.

The attacks on September 11, 2001, are viewed as a physical attack, but they were also an economic attack. From an economic perspective, the attacks achieved several things. First, the level of stock prices dropped. This effectively reduced the wealth of individuals, leading them to spend less on discretionary goods.

Second, uncertainty in the market increased significantly. Uncertainty in financial markets increases the risk in investing, and so increased uncertainty typically makes it more difficult for companies to raise money. This typically results in lower productivity in the overall economy. In the case of 9/11, however, the U.S. economy showed itself to be rather resilient, with productivity leveling off but not falling as many had feared. Recalling our discussion of the capital asset pricing model, increased uncertainty also tends to raise the appropriate discount rate to be used in valuing stocks, and so uncertainty alone typically causes stock prices to fall even if there is ultimately no significant impact on expected cash flows. Figure 8.2 shows the level of the **Dow Jones Industrial Average** (DJIA) over the period January 1990 to March 2011. The immediate effect of the 9/11 attacks was a 14 percent drop in the DJIA, from 9605 on September 10 to 8236 on September 21. Just over a year later, the DJIA bottomed out at 7286, for a total drop (from September 10, 2001) of over 24 percent. Figure 8.3 shows DJIA trading volume over the two-year period from September 11, 2000, to September 11, 2002. As one might expect, trading increased substantially after the attacks, peaking at more than double its normal volume. Figure 8.4 shows the level of the **VIX**, or market volatility index, over the same period. The VIX is a measure of the expected volatility at a specific point in time in the stock market over the subsequent 30-day period. It is derived from the prices of stock options and therefore is determined by supply and demand forces in the marketplace. Figure 8.4 shows a doubling of the VIX from its typical pre-9/11 level to its level immediately after the attacks. Note also that the VIX increased sharply in the days preceding 9/11, rising from 19.71 on August 24, 2001, to 31.84 on September 10, 2001. Some believe that this is compelling evidence that individuals who knew about the impending attacks took action in the markets to profit from them. Figure 8.4 alone does not provide sufficient evidence to draw that conclusion (note that the VIX had exceeded 30 several times over the prior year), but the theory is an interesting one.

Figure 8.2: The Dow Jones Industrial Average

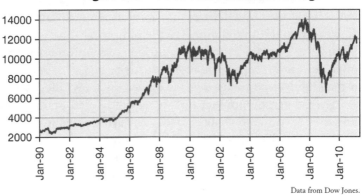

Data from Dow Jones.

Figure 8.3: Dow Jones Industrial Average Volume, September 2000–September 2002

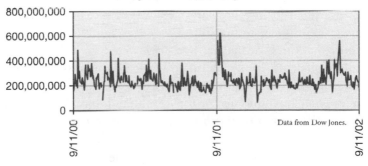

Data from Dow Jones.

Figure 8.4: Expected Stock Market Volatility (VIX)

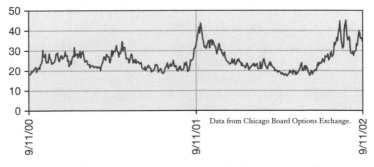

Data from Chicago Board Options Exchange.

As we just noted, some pundits predicted that the 9/11 attacks would throw the United States into a significant recession. After all, we were still suffering from the popping of the dot-com bubble, and the 9/11 attacks surely would have a significant negative impact on travel. Furthermore, productivity had been stagnant in the months leading up to 9/11. Figure 8.5 shows the level of real **gross domestic product** (GDP) in the United States from January 1990 through October 2010. One can see that real GDP was relatively flat from early 2000 through the end of 2001. It is striking that productivity picked up in the aftermath of 9/11 rather than falling. This naturally leads us to ask why productivity did not fall. A variety of factors contributed to the resilience in the economy, but we will mention only a few. Figure 8.6 shows the level of the U.S. **federal funds rate**. The federal funds rate is the government-dictated interest rate charged by member banks on overnight loans to one another, and so it is a key factor in the level of interest rates in the overall economy. Note in the figure that the U.S. Federal Reserve lowered the federal funds rate significantly in the aftermath of the 9/11 attacks. Recalling our discussion of discount rates in Chapter 6, we know that the appropriate discount rate for use in valuing future cash flows is one that is equal to the risk-free rate of return plus a risk premium. As we suggested earlier in this section, the 9/11 attacks created uncertainty in the markets that would have increased the risk premium component of the discount rate. To offset that impact, the Federal Reserve effectively lowered the risk-free rate of interest. That tended to stabilize discount rates, leading to stability in the financial markets.

A second reason for resilience in the U.S. economy was that rates of homeownership were increasing significantly. In 1994, President Bill Clinton directed the U.S. Department of Housing and Urban Development (HUD) to work with housing industry leaders to increase the percentage of people who owned their own homes. Clinton's strategy was termed the National Homeownership Strategy, and its stated goal was to increase rates of home ownership to record levels. President George W. Bush

Figure 8.5: U.S. Real Gross Domestic Product

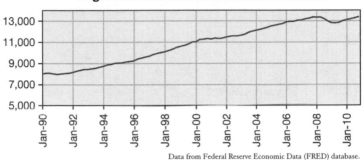

Data from Federal Reserve Economic Data (FRED) database.

Figure 8.6: U.S. Federal Funds Rate

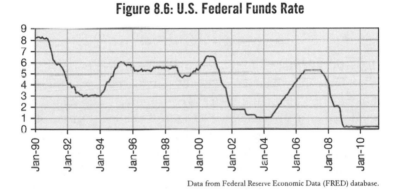

Data from Federal Reserve Economic Data (FRED) database.

shared Clinton's vision and also pushed for increased home ownership. Furthermore, U.S. Federal Reserve Chairman Alan Greenspan, who was chairman under both Clinton and Bush, actively encouraged home ownership in his public speeches. Figure 8.7 shows U.S. home ownership rates from 1980 to the end of 2010. The run-up in ownership rates is obvious. Its importance in the overall economy comes from the building activity that accompanied that run-up. That activity helped stave off the economic pressures resulting from the 9/11 attacks.

The housing effect is important because in retrospect it was a key factor in the subprime mortgage crisis. As Mark Zandi points out in his book *Financial Shock: Global Panic and Government Bailouts—How We Got Here and What Must Be Done to Fix*

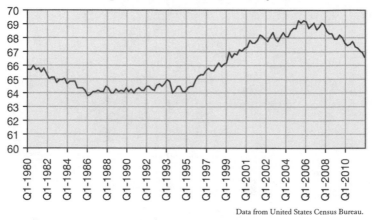

Figure 8.7: U.S. Home Ownership Rate

Data from United States Census Bureau.

It, in the aftermath of 9/11 consumers spent less on travel and more on their own homes (either by purchasing new or different homes or by upgrading their current homes). Those activities tended to push up home prices. Figure 8.8 shows the level of the Case-Shiller Composite-10 Home Price Index, which measures the value of homes in 10 major metropolitan areas. The run-up in home prices was dramatic, with values more than doubling between 2000 and 2006. One reason for that was the effort of Presidents Clinton and Bush to encourage home ownership. Another was the lowering of the federal funds rate in the aftermath of 9/11, which caused mortgage rates to drop. This led not only to an increase in the number of people selling their homes to buy new ones but also to an increase in the number of people who bought run-down homes with the intent of fixing them up and reselling them. These people, called **flippers**, added to the demand for homes, increasing housing prices even more. The impact of flippers became even more pronounced when television shows such as *Sell This House, Designed to Sell,* and *Flip This House* became popular and when the viewership of the cable television network HGTV increased dramatically. Flippers added to the intensity of the housing bubble because they temporarily created demand from one person for two

Figure 8.8: Case-Schiller Home Price Index

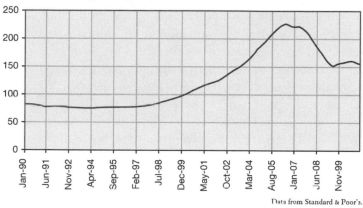

Data from Standard & Poor's.

houses. Furthermore, flippers tended to borrow by taking out second mortgages on their primary homes or by taking out first mortgages on the houses they intended to flip. In either case, the mortgages tended to carry a high interest rate and/or be floating rate in nature. These mortgages are a part of a broader class of mortgages called subprime mortgages because they carry a much higher risk of default than do typical mortgages. We will return to the mortgage crisis later in this chapter but first will discuss a seemingly unrelated event that in retrospect played an important role in the subprime mortgage crisis.

In November 2001, China joined the World Trade Organization (WTO). The WTO was formed in 1995 with the objective of facilitating trade between countries. China's choice to join the WTO was part of a plan to pursue a capitalist economy under a communist government. One result of that development was that China was able to increase its exports of goods quickly. For example, Figure 8.9 shows the trade deficit between China and the United States. The figure shows a dramatic and exponential growth in the net exports of goods from China to the United States. More important, that increase in the supply of goods in the United States created downward pressure on most prices, which effectively kept inflation lower than it would have been otherwise. Although low prices and low inflation ordinarily would seem to be a good thing, the China effect subsequently contributed to a fear of disinflation in the United States, which in turned caused increased uncertainty in the financial markets. Disinflation can be particularly damaging to an economy because consumers generally prefer not to purchase goods today if they believe those goods will be cheaper in the near future. Furthermore, disinflation typically occurs when interest rates are already very low. This reduces the government's ability to stimulate the economy by lowering interest rates.

Because the United States imports more goods from China than it exports to that country, the net currency effect is a transfer of U.S. dollars to Chinese businesses and investors. Those dollars are not of practical use in China, and so the Chinese essentially are forced to spend them in the United States. It follows that as the trade deficit with China increased, Chinese investors acquired more and more financial capital in the United States. Initially, much of that capital, along with capital from other foreign investors, was invested in U.S. Treasury bonds. That demand, along with a lowering of the federal funds rate, tended to increase Treasury bond prices and therefore decrease their returns. Over time, Treasury bonds became less and less attractive and inves-

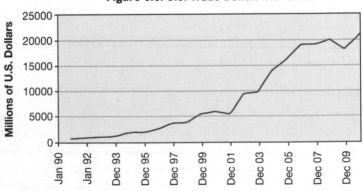

Figure 8.9: U.S. Trade Deficit with China

Data from Federal Reserve Economic Data (FRED) database.

tors began to look at alternatives. Among those alternatives were **mortgage-backed securities** (MBSs). In simple terms, an MBS is a bond that is collateralized by mortgages. MBSs were created through a process called **securitization**, with banks grouping mortgages into pools and then creating securities that were based on those pools. One pool could back an entire series of what are called tranches. Investors in the Class A tranche would receive their money back first, followed by investors in the Class B tranche, and so on. The Class Z tranche would be a residual tranche, with its investors receiving whatever was left over after investors in the other tranches were repaid. Securitization was important to banks because it allowed them to remove mortgages from their balance sheets in exchange for an inflow of cash. That cash could be lent to other borrowers, which earned the banks origination fees. An important aspect of this process was that because a bank did not retain the mortgages, it had a reduced incentive to screen borrowers thoroughly.

I believe there were five main factors of the real estate crisis: (1) the government encouragement of home ownership, (2) the Federal Reserve's policy of low interest rates, (3) international growth, which led to high liquidity in the marketplace, (4) the emergence of residential mortgage-backed securities, and (5) weak credit analysis of securitized packages.

—Don Childress
Senior Managing Partner
Childress Klein Properties

Ratings agencies (e.g., Moody's, Standard & Poor's, Fitch) play an important role in the securitization process because they provide certifications of the quality of the securities being offered. Those certifications take the form of letter-based grades that, roughly speaking, correspond to the likelihoods of default for the various securities. The ratings for MBSs were particularly high in the early 2000s, perhaps because of the fact that real estate prices consistently had trended upward for more than five decades. As long as that trend continued, the mortgage principal presumably could be recovered in the foreclosure process if the borrower defaulted. With that belief in mind, it was easy to rationalize higher ratings for securities that were backed by mortgages. Furthermore, insurance on MBSs was incredibly cheap because of the high ratings and the low likelihood that housing prices would fall.

The increased capital flow into the MBS market created not just higher demand for the securities but also higher demand for the mortgages that supported them. This gave mortgage brokers and banks an extra incentive to generate more mortgages. After all, both the mortgage brokers and the banks were essentially earning money from the fees charged when a mortgage was originated. Of course, finding more people to take out mortgages was becoming increasingly difficult because there were minimum standards a borrower had to meet to be eligible for a mortgage. For example, on a standard mortgage, the mortgage payment could not exceed 28 percent of the borrower's gross monthly income and the borrower's total monthly debt payments could not exceed 36 percent of the borrower's gross monthly income. This meant that to originate more mortgages, banks would have to either decrease the monthly payment or increase the borrower's income. To decrease the monthly payment, banks created interest-only mortgages and interest-only adjustable-rate mortgages (ARMs). In requiring the borrower to cover only the interest obligation and not pay down the principal, the bank was counting on housing prices continuing to climb as they had over the last half century. As long as they did, the bank could count on receiving the principal at some unspecified future date when the house was sold. Eventually, though, the demand for interest-only loans was essentially exhausted, and banks took things a step further by creating option ARMs. In an option ARM, the borrower must choose a payment that is above some specified minimum, but that minimum is below the interest-only level. Choosing a payment below the interest-only level essentially entails a negative payment on the mortgage principal, and so the mortgage balance will grow over time. From the bank's perspective, this is fine as long as the property value grows at a greater rate than does the mortgage balance. Of course, when property values fall, the borrower quickly goes upside down (i.e., owes more than the property is worth) and the mortgage drops significantly in value.

To address the income side of the qualification requirements, banks, led by Ameriquest Mortgage, created stated income loans, which later became known as liar loans. Stated income loans are ones in which the lender does not verify the income level of borrowers. Although such loans may be useful in situations in which it is difficult for borrowers to document their income, they are flawed in that borrowers can lie about their incomes to borrow more money (for example, I know a woman in Florida who managed to take out a $300,000 mortgage with only $26,000 in annual income).

In retrospect, the banking innovations designed to make more and more people eligible for mortgages were a devastating factor in the subprime mortgage crisis. Still, banks do not deserve all the blame for the debacle. As real estate prices climbed in the early 2000s, the U.S. Federal Reserve actively encouraged people

Indeed, recent research within the Federal Reserve suggests that many homeowners might have saved tens of thousands of dollars had they held adjustable-rate mortgages rather than fixed-rate mortgages during the past decade, though this would not have been the case, of course, had interest rates trended sharply upward.

—Alan Greenspan
U.S. Federal Reserve Chairman
February 2004

> Improvements in lending practices driven by information technology have enabled lenders to reach out to households with previously unrecognized borrowing capacities.
>
> —Alan Greenspan
> U.S. Federal Reserve Chairman
> October 2004

not only to take out mortgages but to take out adjustable-rate mortgages, which provide a low initial payment but have the risk that payments will increase substantially in the future. Furthermore, the Federal Reserve all but explicitly endorsed the innovations in mortgage products by touting them publicly.

Looking back, it is clear that both the Federal Reserve and most other housing experts simply did not anticipate the collapse on any real level. The earliest public indications that U.S. economic leaders suspected there might be a problem did not come until late in 2005, but by that time it was too late for corrective measures to be effective. In retrospect, it is easy to blame those leaders, but the reality is that there is a long economic history both in the United States and abroad that includes numerous bubbles. The very nature of bubbles is that they tend to

> I don't foresee any national decline in home price values. Freddie Mac's analysis of single-family houses over the last half century hasn't shown a single year when the national average housing price has gone down. The last consistent drop was during the Great Depression, when the unemployment rate got up to 25 percent, or five times the level we're at now.
>
> —Frank Nothaft
> Freddie Mac Chief Economist
> *BusinessWeek*, June 22, 2005

The apparent froth in housing markets may have spilled over into mortgage markets. The dramatic increase in the prevalence of interest-only loans, as well as the introduction of other, more-exotic forms of adjustable-rate mortgages, are developments that bear close scrutiny.

—Alan Greenspan
U.S. Federal Reserve Chairman
September 2005

be obvious in hindsight but unintentionally disguised as they happen.

The housing bubble lasted for a few years, but like all bubbles it eventually collapsed. This is evident in Figure 8.8, which shows a significant drop in home values in 2007 and 2008. Interestingly, values today are much higher than they were in 2000, suggesting that values may decline further before reaching a natural equilibrium.

The impact of the bubble was far reaching, leading to a dramatic increase in unemployment, with rates that remain high to this day. Figure 8.10 shows the unemployment rate from 1990 through the beginning of 2011. Despite the decline in 2011,

Figure 8.10: U.S. Unemployment Rate

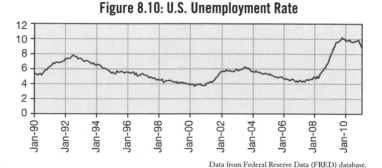

Data from Federal Reserve Data (FRED) database.

unemployment rates remain at extremely high levels. Furthermore, unemployment rates are much higher in some areas. For example, the U.S. Bureau of Labor Statistics reported that the February 2011 unemployment rates in Florida and Nevada were 11 percent and 13.6 percent, respectively. Any meaningful recovery will be one in which these rates (and the nationwide rate) drop significantly and in which the housing market stabilizes at a sustainable equilibrium. Currently, neither of those things seems to be imminent.

CHAPTER 9

SUGGESTED READINGS

Financial firms want to hire people who are intellectually curious and have a demonstrated interest in finance. An easy way for an interviewer to test both of these ideas is to generate a discussion with the candidate about books the candidate has read. In addition, firms want to hire candidates who have a solid working knowledge of what goes on in the financial world. For both of these reasons, job candidates should devote a portion of their spare time to reading popular and influential books that are related to finance. With that in mind, the following books are highly recommended for anyone who wants to work in finance. Keep in mind that the list is far from exhaustive. There are many other books that would serve a job candidate's purposes quite well. The important thing is for candidates to read relevant material so that they can build a body of knowledge to draw on during interviews. Having said that, those who have not been intellectually curious enough to have made financial readings a regular part of their free time should question whether they should go to work on Wall Street. Entry-level jobs there can be particularly difficult, and only those with a real passion for the field tend to do well.

Students often ask which books they should read first. Although all the books listed here are worthwhile, two of them stand out as being particularly useful for someone who will be interviewing for a position in financial services. The first is Burton Malkiel's *A Random Walk down Wall Street,* which is such

> My advice—be authentic, show a genuine commitment to the profession, and ask yourself if you are ready for a Wall Street gig before you interview. Otherwise, you are stealing a valuable spot from someone else.
>
> —Akshat Shah
> Director in Healthcare Investment Banking
> UBS

an iconic book that virtually every financial analyst on Wall Street has read it. For that reason alone, job candidates should read it. The second is Mark Zandi's *Financial Shock: Global Panic and Government Bailouts—How We Got Here and What Must Be Done to Fix It,* which is a rather clear exposition on the causes of the real estate crisis. Beyond those two, there is no particular recommended order for reading the books.

RECOMMENDED READINGS

A Random Walk down Wall Street by Burton Malkiel: The thesis of Malkiel's book is that it is very difficult for anyone, let alone the average investor, to beat the market on a consistent basis. To make his point, Malkiel takes the reader on a fascinating journey through anecdotal and statistical evidence that supports his thesis. Perhaps more than any other book, people interested in working in finance are expected to have read Malkiel's book. If a job candidate has not read the book, interviewers will wonder whether the candidate really wants to work in finance.

Against the Gods: The Remarkable Story of Risk by Peter Bernstein: Bernstein traces the history of risk management in an effort to illustrate its importance in nearly every part of society. The lessons of the book are widespread, among them being the importance of understanding uncertainty and the value of building on the work of others. Like Bernstein's *Capital Ideas,* this is not as light a read as some of the others on this list. Still, it is highly regarded by many on Wall Street and therefore should be read by anyone interested in working there.

The Big Short: Inside the Doomsday Machine and **Liar's Poker: Rising through the Wreckage on Wall Street** by Michael Lewis: Lewis is a former investment banker who has become well-known for writing several books, including *Moneyball: The Art of Winning an Unfair Game* and *The Blind Side* (which was made into an Oscar-winning film of the same name). In *The Big Short,* Lewis takes a look at specific individuals who played a role in the real estate crisis. In doing so, he seeks to understand who knew about the impending crisis at what points in time. Like Lewis's other books, *The Big Short* is highly entertaining and a very easy read. It also gives the reader a great deal of insight into what went wrong in the early 2000s. In *Liar's Poker,* Lewis talks about his experiences while working as a banker as Salomon Brothers. The book is humorous yet gives the reader an inside look at the life of an investment banker.

Capital Ideas: The Improbable Origins of Modern Wall Street by Peter Bernstein: Bernstein writes for a somewhat sophisticated audience with a strong knowledge of market economics, examining how academic research has revolutionized some of the financial approaches used on Wall Street. The book is a more difficult read than many of the others on this list, but it is worthwhile nonetheless.

Den of Thieves by James Stewart: Stewart recounts the story of Michael Milken, Ivan Boesky, and others who conspired to trade securities by using inside information. The story is a compelling look at how temptation and greed led to one of

Wall Street's biggest scandals. The book also gives readers an inside look at life on Wall Street, and so job candidates are well advised to read it.

Financial Shenanigans: How to Detect Accounting Gimmicks and Fraud in Financial Reports by Howard Schilit: In contrast to the other books on this list, Schilit deals with issues an analyst might face regularly on the job. Managers of corporations (particularly publicly held ones) have incentives to mislead outsiders, and Schilit examines the ways in which those managers might use accounting gimmicks to make a company appear to be in better financial shape than it really is. Job candidates who find an opportunity to explain one of these gimmicks in an interview can greatly improve their chances of getting the job.

Financial Shock: Global Panic and Government Bailouts—How We Got Here and What Must Be Done to Fix It by Mark Zandi: Zandi is the chief economist for Moody's Analytics and is widely and highly regarded in the financial community. In *Financial Shock,* he carefully and methodically lays out the causes of the subprime mortgage crisis and then outlines his thoughts on how to hasten the recovery. In doing so, he gives a job candidate ample ammunition to use in an interview. In contrast to Lewis's *The Big Short,* Zandi takes a big picture look at the crisis. Because interviews for financial jobs often turn to the candidate's knowledge about and understanding of the recent real estate crisis, *Financial Shock* is a must-read for anyone interested in working in finance.

Fooled by Randomness and *The Black Swan: The Impact of the Highly Improbable* by Nassim Nicholas Taleb: Taleb has similar theses in both books. His objective is to encourage the reader to maintain a healthy skepticism about empirical work. To meet that objective, he takes the reader through a series of historical stories that illustrate his points. The books are highly entertaining and as a result are very easy to read. If there is one overarching theme of the books, it is that people tend to place too much emphasis on historical events and therefore overestimate the likelihood that they will repeat themselves. The sort of skepticism that Taleb encourages is highly valued on Wall Street, and so Taleb's books should be high on the reading list of anyone interested in working in finance.

Latticework: The New Investing by Robert Hagstrom: Hagstrom is a portfolio manager for Legg Mason Capital Management (LMCM). One philosophy of LMCM is that one can learn a great deal about how financial markets behave by studying seemingly unrelated disciplines. In *Latticework,* Hagstrom briefly reviews some of the main ideas from physics, psychology, biology, literature, and other disciplines in an effort to draw parallels with successful investing.

The Psychology of Investing by John Nofsinger: Nofsinger summarizes some of the research on behavioral finance and offers examples to support his claims. The book provides an interesting look at the role psychology and other disciplines play in financial markets.

Reminiscences of a Stock Operator by Edwin Lefèvre: Although a relatively old book (written in the 1920s), this book more than any other is a must-read for anyone interested in sales and trading; it also is highly recommended for anyone else who wants to work on Wall Street. In this highly entertaining read, Lefèvre recounts the story of Larry Livingston (a pseudonym for Jesse Livermore), who made his fortune by trading stocks in the early 1900s. Although today's financial world differs dramatically from the world Livermore traded in, many of Livermore's beliefs are applicable today. For a job candidate interviewing for a sales and trading position, there is perhaps no better answer to the question "What have you been reading lately?" than to cite *Reminiscences of a Stock Operator.*

When Genius Failed: The Rise and Fall of Long-Term Capital Management by Roger Lowenstein: Lowenstein recounts the story of a group of financial geniuses (including Nobel Prize winners) who formed a hedge fund company called Long-Term Capital Management (LTCM). LTCM ultimately failed because its managers failed to understand the implications of seemingly insignificant differences between theory and practice. Although few people in the general public realized it at the time, the collapse of LTCM placed enormous strain on the U.S. financial system. That triggered emergency meetings among the most powerful people in the financial world in an effort to handle the crisis. Like several other books on this list, *When Genius Failed* documents a legendary event in financial history and is therefore recommended reading for anyone interested in working in finance.

OTHER RESOURCES

The Internet is of course a convenient and sometimes fantastic source of information, but candidates should use it cautiously. The Vault (http://www.vault.com) is probably the single best Internet resource for those interested in a career on Wall Street. It provides information on the banks themselves as well advice on cover letters and résumés. It also provides a Vault Career Guide for virtually every segment of the finance world.

Job candidates interested in gaining a more in-depth understanding of how finance is applied in the real world should consider taking courses in finance and should consider any of a number of books on the subject. Candidates interested in learning more about the types of questions interviewers might consult Tim Crack's *Heard on the Street: Quantitative Questions from Basic Wall Street Interviews*, although students should note that the book covers questions that are well beyond those that undergraduate candidates might be asked.

GLOSSARY
of Financial Terms

································►

Beta: A measure of the nondiversifiable risk associated with an asset. Assets with negative betas are negatively correlated with the market, whereas those with positive betas are positively correlated with the market.

Book value: The accounting value of an asset or liability as it appears on the balance sheet. Assets and liabilities initially are recorded on the balance sheet at their cost (or their market value at that time), but over time market values tend to diverge from book values. This means that the book value can be a very poor estimate of market value, particularly for assets and liabilities that have been on the books for a long period.

Buy side: A segment of the financial services industry consisting of institutional investors that manage portfolios of assets on behalf of other investors.

Capital structure: The composition of a company's debt, preferred stock, and common stock.

Commercial bank: A financial institution that collects deposits from individual and corporate savers and invests those deposits, typically by granting loans to individuals and companies.

Core school: A college or university that is specifically targeted by a firm to recruit students. A typical investment bank will maintain a list of about 10 core schools and spend money to send a recruiting team to campus to hold information sessions, host dinners, and conduct interviews.

Debt: A liability with prespecified payments to be paid on prespecified dates. Debtholders essentially lend money to companies in exchange for those promised payments. If the company defaults on the debt, debtholders may be able to seize its assets in lieu of the missed payments.

Discount rate: An interest rate used in time value of money formulas to adjust the value of future cash flows for the opportunity cost associated with not receiving the cash flows earlier. In theory, the discount rate should be equal to the expected return on alternative securities with equivalent risk.

Diversifiable risk: Risk associated with a particular asset that becomes insignificant if the asset is held in a well-diversified portfolio. For example, any company-specific risk becomes negligible if an investor holds the company's stock in a portfolio with many other stocks.

Dividend: A type of payment from a company to its shareholders. The amount of a preferred stock dividend is prespecified, whereas the amount of a common stock dividend is entirely at the discretion of company managers.

Dot-com bubble: A period during the late 1900s (sometimes dated as 1995–2000) in which the prices of technology-related stocks rose to seemingly irrational levels only to fall precipitously in the early 2000s (2000–2003).

Dow Jones Industrial Average: A stock market index that reflects the price level of 30 large publicly traded stocks in the United

States. Although the index historically tracked industrial stocks, in recent years it has expanded its scope to include stocks such as Microsoft and Verizon.

Earnings before interest and taxes (EBIT): A measure of the money generated by a firm during a specific period that is available to compensate debtholders, the government, and equityholders. EBIT usually is reported on the company's income statement and is used as an element of the DCF valuation approach.

Earnings before interest, taxes, depreciation, and amortization (EBITDA): A measure of the money generated by a firm during a specific period that is available to compensate debtholders, the government, and equityholders. In contrast to EBIT, EBITDA does not take into account D&A expenses because they are non–cash flow expenses. As a result, EBITDA generally is considered a better measure of cash flow than EBIT. EBITDA is a commonly used measure in the trading comps and transaction comps valuation approaches.

Enterprise value (EV): An estimate of the value of a company's entire operations, not just the portion owned by shareholders. EV, which is also called *firm value*, is the sum of the market values of a company's net debt, preferred stock, and common stock. It is used commonly in the trading comps, transaction comps, and DCF valuation approaches.

Equity: The residual claim on company assets and cash flows. "Residual" in this case means that equityholders (often called shareholders) have the right to firm cash flows after all other claimants (e.g., employees, trade creditors, debtholders, governments) have been paid.

Exploding offer: A job offer in which the candidate is given a restrictively short period to respond. Although there is no specific rule defining what is or is not an exploding offer, any offer expiring in less than a week or two might reasonably be called an exploding one.

Federal funds rate: The government-mandated interest rate charged by member banks on overnight loans to one another. In theory, a higher federal funds rate increases the banks' costs, leading them to pass those costs on to borrowers. Because of that, the federal funds rate represents a key tool that the U.S. Federal Reserve can use in its efforts to control the economy.

Flipper: An individual or organization that buys housing properties and fixes them up in hopes of selling them for a profit.

Free cash flow (FCF): A measure of the actual cash flow generated by a company over a specific period, excluding any cash flows related to the company's financing, such as dividends, interest payments, issuances of debt or equity, and retirement of debt or equity.

Gross domestic product (GDP): A measure of the value of the goods and services generated by a particular economy over a specific period.

Initial public offering (IPO): The first public offering of a company's stock. An IPO typically is executed by an investment bank, with the bank becoming at least a temporary owner of some portion of the company's stock.

Investment bank: A financial institution that acts as intermediary between investors and organizations that need financing. Its primary functions include corporate finance, sales and trading, wealth management, and research.

Market maker: An entity that both buys and sells a particular security to provide liquidity to the specific market. Market makers make money by buying at a price below the price at which they sell.

Market multiple: The ratio of some measure of the market value of a company or the company's stock to some measure of a factor that contributes to the market value. Multiples such as the P/E ratio and the EV/EBITDA ratio are used commonly on Wall Street.

Market risk premium: A key component of the capital asset pricing model. The market risk premium measures the additional return investors need above the risk-free rate of return to invest in the market.

Market value: The amount of money it would take to purchase all of an outstanding security issuance at the current market price. For example, the market value of a company's stock is the current stock price multiplied by the number of shares outstanding.

Mortgage-backed security (MBS): A security for which investors receive a specified series of cash flows that are based on the cash flows of the mortgages that constitute the security. Often, one pool of mortgages will back multiple MBSs. In addition, most MBSs are guaranteed by entities such as Fannie Mae and Freddie Mac.

Net debt: The value of a company's debt minus the amount of cash the company has on hand. Intuitively, the company could use the cash to pay down the debt at any time, and so net debt is a measure of the additional money the company would need to generate to repay all of the debt.

Nondiversifiable risk: The risk associated with an asset that cannot be eliminated even if the investor holds a well-diversified portfolio. For example, all companies are affected by changes in interest rates, and so an investor generally cannot eliminate interest rate risk through diversification.

Perpetual growth: A cash flow structure in which each successive cash flow is higher than the previous one by a fixed percentage that does not vary over time.

Perpetuity: An annuity that has an infinite life.

Private equity: A segment of the financial services industry that focuses on equity ownership of private companies. Private equity shops buy stock in privately held companies or buy a controlling interest in a publicly held company and take it private. The latter is what is known as a *leveraged buyout*

(LBO). Private equity shops often take an active role in the management of the companies in which they invest, hoping to add value by improving the efficiency of those companies.

Return: The percentage change in the value of an investment over a specified period.

Risk-free rate: The interest rate on a security that has no risk. In other words, it is the interest rate on a security for which both the timing and the amount of the future cash flows are certain.

Securitization: A process by which financial institutions combine financial assets (often small in magnitude) to create other financial assets with desired characteristics. For example, a pool of mortgages might be combined to create a series of securities with different risk-return characteristics.

Sell side: A segment of the financial services industry consisting of those who engage in research and/or sell securities on behalf of others.

Spread: The profit earned by a financial intermediary that buys securities and then sells them. The intermediary's objective is to sell a security at a higher price than the price at which it bought the security, earning the difference as compensation for providing liquidity to the market.

Stated income loan: A loan in which the lender does not verify the income of the borrower. Because borrowers are aware of this practice, they can lie about their incomes in an effort to obtain a larger mortgage. For this reason, these loans often are called liar loans. Of course, lenders recognize this and as a result charge high interest rates on these loans.

Terminal value: The value as of the forecast horizon of any cash flows that may be received after the forecast horizon. The forecast horizon is simply the last date for which the analyst has explicitly forecast a cash flow.

VIX: A measure of the volatility expected in the stock market over the coming month. The level of the VIX is determined by the implied volatility in option prices on the S&P 500 Index.

Weighted average cost of capital (WACC): A measure of the return a company must generate to satisfy all of its capital market investors: debtholders, preferred stockholders, and common stockholders.

Yield to maturity: The implied interest rate on a bond, assuming that all the bond cash flows will be paid in full as scheduled.

BIBLIOGRAPHY

Bernstein, Peter L. *Against the Gods: The Remarkable Story of Risk.* Wiley, 1998.

Bernstein, Peter L. *Capital Ideas: The Improbable Origins of Modern Wall Street.* Wiley, 2005.

Crack, Timothy. *Heard on the Street: Quantitative Questions from Basic Wall Street Interviews,* 12th ed. Timothy Falcon Crack, 2001.

Fox, Jeffrey J. *How to Land Your Dream Job: No Resume! And Other Secrets to Get You in the Door.* Hyperion, 2007.

Hagstrom, Robert G. *Latticework: The New Investing.* Texere, 2000.

Hoover, Scott. *Stock Valuation: An Essential Guide to Wall Street's Most Popular Valuation Models.* McGraw-Hill, 2005.

Lefèvre, Edwin. *Reminiscences of a Stock Operator,* foreword by Roger Lowenstein. Wiley, 2006.

Lewis, Michael. *The Big Short: Inside the Doomsday Machine.* W. W. Norton, 2010.

Lewis, Michael. *Liar's Poker*. W. W. Norton, 1989.

Lowenstein, Roger. *When Genius Failed: The Rise and Fall of Long-Term Capital Management*. Random House, 2001.

Malkiel, Burton G. *A Random Walk down Wall Street: The Time-Tested Strategy for Successful Investing*. W. W. Norton, 1973.

Nofsinger, John R. *The Psychology of Investing*. Prentice Hall, 2010.

Schilit, Howard M. *Financial Shenanigans: How to Detect Accounting Gimmicks & Fraud in Financial Reports*. McGraw-Hill, 2010.

Stewart, James B. *Den of Thieves*. Touchstone, 1992.

Taleb, Nassim N. *The Black Swan: The Impact of the Highly Improbable*. Random House, 2010.

Taleb, Nassim N. *Fooled by Randomness: The Hidden Role of Chance in Life and in the Markets*. Random House, 2008.

Zandi, Mark. *Financial Shock: Global Panic and Government Bailouts—How We Got Here and What Must Be Done to Fix It*. Pearson, 2009.

INDEX

ABOUT THE AUTHOR

Scott Hoover is an associate professor of finance at Washington and Lee University. He teaches a variety of finance courses, including corporate finance, multinational corporate finance, investments, and real estate finance. Scott served for eight years as advisor to the Williams Investment Society.

Scott is the author of *Stock Valuation: An Essential Guide to Wall Street's Most Popular Valuation Models.* He has also been a frequent guest on both television and radio shows, including programs on ABC, CNN, Fox News, Fox Business Channel, NBC and NPR.

Scott lives in Lexington, Virginia.